Matt Chandler

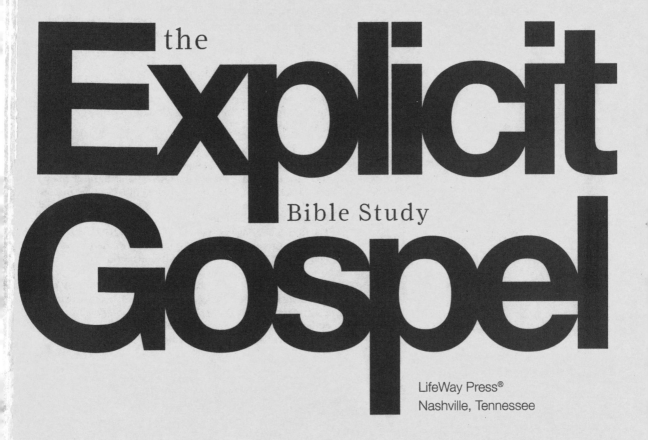

the
Explicit

Bible Study

Gospel

LifeWay Press®
Nashville, Tennessee

Published by LifeWay Press® • © 2012 Matt Chandler
Reprinted 2018

ISBN 978-1-4158-7362-5 • Item 005500792

Dewey decimal classification: 234
Subject headings: BIBLE. N.T. GOSPELS \
CHRISTIAN LIFE \ GOD

To order additional copies of this resource, write to LifeWay
Resources Customer Service; One LifeWay Plaza; Nashville,
TN 37234; fax 615-251-5933; phone toll free 800-458-2772; order
online at LifeWay.com; email orderentry@lifeway.com; or visit
the LifeWay Christian Store serving you.

Printed in the United States of America

Groups Ministry Publishing • LifeWay Resources
One LifeWay Plaza • Nashville, TN 37234

Contents

The Author

Matt Chandler serves as the lead pastor of teaching at The Village Church in Flower Mound, Texas. Having served in that role since December 2002, he describes his tenure at The Village as a replanting effort to change the theological and philosophical culture of the congregation. The church has witnessed a tremendous response, growing from 160 people to more than 10,000, with satellite campuses in Flower Mound, Dallas, and Denton.

Alongside his current role as lead pastor, Matt is involved in church-planting efforts both locally and internationally through The Village and various strategic partnerships. Prior to accepting the pastorate at The Village, Matt had a vibrant itinerant ministry for more than 10 years that gave him the opportunity to speak to thousands of people in America and abroad about the glory of God and the beauty of Jesus.

Recently, Matt was named the president of Acts 29, a worldwide church-planting organization. Over the past 10 years Acts 29 has emerged from a small band of brothers to more than four hundred churches in the United States and networks of churches in multiple countries.

Other than knowing Jesus, Matt's greatest joy is being married to Lauren and being the dad to their three children, Audrey, Reid, and Norah.

Introduction

Once I heard several new believers tell the stories of how they were saved. I was a little surprised by what I heard. One after another, each person told some variation of the same story: "I grew up in church; we were there every time the doors were open. I was baptized when I was six, seven, or eight but didn't understand what the gospel was. After a while I lost interest in church and Jesus, and I started walking in open sin. Someone recently sat me down and explained the gospel to me for the first time. I was blown away. No one ever taught me that."

For the first time I asked myself, *How can you grow up going to church every week and not hear the gospel?* After having a few conversations, I concluded that those people who had once walked away from the gospel hadn't heard the real gospel at all. Rather, they had accepted a perversion of the gospel claiming that after they were saved, they were on our own, responsible for earning favor with God and justifying themselves before Him through good behavior. The emphasis was on being good and avoiding bad, not on a God who redeems and sustains. The gospel had been assumed, not taught or proclaimed as central. It hadn't been explicit.

For some reason we think although the cross saves us from past sin, then we have to take over and clean ourselves up after we are saved. This thinking is devastating to the soul. In 1 Corinthians 15:1-5 Paul reminded the Corinthians that they were saved by the gospel, would be sustained by it, and were currently standing in it. Thinking we can abandon our Savior along our spiritual journey and go back to self-reliance is idolatry. Elsewhere Paul taught that even religious effort is worthless compared to the surpassing greatness of Christ (see Phil. 3:4-9). If we add to or subtract from the cross, we rob God of His glory and Christ of His sufficiency.

Romans 8:1 says there is no condemnation for us, not because of the great stuff we've done but because Christ has set us free from the law of sin and death. We are saved, sanctified, and sustained by what Jesus did for us on the cross and through the power of His resurrection. Our past sin, our current struggles, and our future failures are paid in full by the marvelous, infinite, matchless grace found in the atoning work of the cross of Jesus Christ.

Over the next six weeks I want to challenge you to grasp the centrality of the gospel for all of the Christian life, from the moment of salvation, through the lifelong process of sanctification, and continuing into eternity. We'll see how the glory of God reigns supreme over every moment in His plan for our lives and how the cross captures and resurrects our dead hearts. We'll also see that the gospel is not just personal but cosmic. Christ's atoning work reveals God's plan of redemption from the beginning of time to the end of time. The gospel fulfills the longing of all creation to be made new in Christ.

I pray that through this study, you will glimpse the size and weight of the good news, the eternity-spanning glory of the finished work of Christ.

Week 1
The Gospel of Past, Present, and Future

Start

Welcome to your first small-group discussion of *The Explicit Gospel*. Begin the session with the activity below.

Several words in the English language have multiple definitions and uses. For example, the word *strike* can refer to both hitting something (in a fight) and missing something (in a baseball game).

Take a minute to think of a word that has multiple definitions. Write down as many of those definitions as you can think of in three to five minutes. At the end of the allotted time, consider sharing the results of your work with the rest of the group.

What first comes to mind when you hear the word *gospel?*

What are different definitions and uses of the word *gospel* in today's culture? In the church?

Watch

Complete the viewer guide below as you view DVD session 1.

Paul is just as concerned with _____ understanding the gospel as he is with non-Christians understanding the gospel.

The gospel is not simply for those who _____ _____ know Christ, but it's just as much for those who _____ know Christ.

You were saved by _____ the gospel.

So much of our lack of holiness goes back to a misunderstanding of the gospel and what it means to _____ in the gospel _____.

When we stand up to _____ and we don't give in to our flesh, that's standing in the gospel.

To persevere to the end, you constantly preach the gospel to _____.

God wove delight in our _____ into the fabric of creation to remind us of His deep and abiding _____ in us in Jesus Christ.

The gospel sustains us. We just have to _____ it sustains us.

God works in the middle of _____.

God is making much of _____ in our salvation.

Your right standing before God is not built on you but on _____ _____.

Video sessions available for purchase at *lifeway.com/explicitgospel*

Respond

Discuss the DVD segment with your group, using the questions below.

What struck you as new or interesting in the DVD segment?

Look at the definition you wrote earlier for the word *gospel*. What changes, if any, would you make to that definition after hearing Matt speak?

Do you agree that the gospel applies to those who know Christ as much as it applies to those who still need to experience salvation? Why or why not?

Summarize what it means to stand in the gospel as a follower of Jesus.

How would you describe your current understanding and practice of the gospel: crawling like a wounded soldier, taking your first steps, walking confidently, or running?

What obstacles or attitudes are holding you back from advancing in your understanding and practice of the gospel?

Identify one action you could take this week to move beyond those obstacles and attitudes. If you're willing, share that action with the group.

Suggested Scripture memory for this week: 1 CORINTHIANS 15:1-2

Now brothers, I want to clarify for you the gospel I proclaimed to you; you received it and have taken your stand on it. You are also saved by it, if you hold to the message I proclaimed to you—unless you believed for no purpose.

Read week 1 and complete the activities before the next group experience.

What is most
important in the
Christian life?

The answer might
be tougher to
pin down than
you think.

The Gospel of Past, Present, and Future

If an outsider to the faith wanted to answer that question and surveyed evangelical churches to learn the focal point of their teachings, what would he find? He might find that the most important thing is behavior. Sunday after Sunday behavioral dictums are handed down from the pulpit in an effort to create well-mannered citizens. Or he might find that the answer is heaven and hell. Every week pastors extol the virtues and declare the terrors of eternal life or eternal death. Or he might find that the most important thing in Christianity is how to live better—to become wealthier, healthier, and better husbands, wives, children, and employees.

But if you asked the apostle Paul that question, he wouldn't waver. In 1 Corinthians 15:3-4 he clearly recorded for us what is most important in the Christian life.

It's the gospel.

What Is the Gospel?

The gospel is making a comeback. Have you noticed?

It's pretty popular right now in evangelical circles to talk about the gospel. From books to blogs, conferences to DVDs, there is a call back to what Paul called "most important" (1 Cor. 15:3). But with all this talk about the gospel, there comes a tendency to use the word without really understanding what it means.

In fact, there are false gospels today, just as in Paul's day. That's why our understanding of, belief in, and proclamation of the gospel must be explicit. We'd better be talking about the same thing Paul and the other biblical authors wrote about when the gospel is mentioned in Scripture.

In a few sentences, what is the gospel?

Read Galatians 1:6-9. What did Paul say should happen to those who preach a false gospel?

Does that seem extreme to you? Why or why not?

The gospel was no laughing matter to Paul. Here the same man who wished he could go to hell on behalf of his unbelieving Jewish countrymen said those who don't preach the explicit gospel should be cursed—eternally condemned. And in case you didn't get it the first time, he said it again for emphasis: "As we have said before, I now say again: If anyone preaches to you a gospel contrary to what you received, a curse be on him!" (Gal. 1:9).

Are you starting to see it? The gospel—the undiluted, unchanging, explicit gospel—is the foundation for everything. We need to get it right.

What are some ways our culture changes the gospel today?

How do churches add to the gospel?

What methods have you tried?

How might you guard against incorporating an altered gospel into your own faith?

In the Book of Galatians, some teachers in the church were advocating a grace-plus system. They argued that the cross of Jesus Christ and the grace of God were a great place to begin, but if you really wanted to be acceptable to God, you needed to progress from there. You had to observe certain religious days of the year, eat a certain way, and be circumcised. Those might seem like small things, but these subtle variances corrupted the good news of grace.

These efforts are self-reliance instead of God-reliance. The idolatry in the human heart always wants to lead us away from our Savior and back to self-reliance, no matter how pitiful that self-reliance is. All your church attendance, your religious activities, your Sunday School attendance pins, your journals, and your quiet times—it's all in vain if you don't have Christ.

Read 1 Corinthians 15:1-8. Record the essential message of the gospel, according to Paul.

There isn't much wiggle room in this passage. Christ died for our sins. He was buried and rose again. And all this happened according to God's plan. That's the gospel. It's not Jesus plus our best effort. The gospel is centered on the work of Christ and His work alone.

But something else in this passage is instructive for us too. Somewhere along the line, we started thinking the gospel is strictly about heaven and hell—the means by which we get out of one and into the other. In other words, the purpose of the gospel is for when we die. But look back at verses 1-2, and you'll see a dramatically different viewpoint.

Based on 1 Corinthians 15:1-2, did Paul see the gospel as applicable only when we die? How do you know?

If we think of the gospel as applying only to our eternal destiny, we are short-changing the death of Christ in a dramatic way. According to Paul, the gospel isn't only for the lost; the gospel is also for the saved. It's not only for when you die but also for every day of your life. In fact, the only way someone can truly live the kind of life Jesus intended is to understand that the gospel is for your past, present, and future. It's the means by which you are saved, are made holy, and are preserved until the end.

Is the gospel the center point of your entire life, or have you relegated it to a certain part of your past, present, or future?

PRAY THE WORDS OF PAUL IN 1 CORINTHIANS 15:1-8 TODAY. PRAY FOR GOD TO REVEAL HOW YOU CAN LIVE A TRULY GOSPEL-CENTERED LIFE AS YOU COMPLETE THIS STUDY.

The Gospel Saves You

"When did you get saved?"

Maybe it's a southern thing, but in the Bible Belt you can scarcely find a single person who hasn't heard that question. Most people actually have an answer too. But maybe the question has been asked so many times that we've forgotten the underlying assumption: in order to be saved, you must have been in great danger at one time. Even many people who can answer the question with a specific date and time don't feel the sense of impending doom that awaited them before they were saved. But the gospel can help us with that.

Have you ever been asked the previous question? How would you answer it?

What were you saved from?

How does knowing the answer to that question help you love and appreciate the gospel?

The short answer is hell; that's what the gospel saves us from. Though accurate, that answer is nonetheless a bit incomplete, especially in today's culture, where it's becoming increasingly unpopular to talk much about hell. But if it's not popular to talk about hell, Jesus would certainly have a hard time fitting into our religious context.

He wasn't floating around like a mystical Ghandi, never angry at anybody. He talked about hell. A lot.

Read the following passages and record what each communicates about the nature of hell.
Matthew 8:12
Matthew 18:8-9
Mark 9:48
Revelation 14:11

Based on these passages, do you think Jesus thought more or less about hell than you do?

What value might there be in thinking about the reality of hell?

The reality of hell is terrifying. Ironically, though, it's really terrifying only to those who are being saved from it. That is to say, people bound for hell by and large don't believe it exists, and that makes the danger all the more real and disturbing. It's one thing to be scared because you know a lion is lurking in front of you; it's another thing to simply walk through the jungle unaware of the poisonous snake that is silently slithering at your feet.

We desperately need to be saved. Yet we are so far gone that apart from the work of God, we don't even realize we need to be saved. That's the true condition of humankind.

Read Ephesians 2:1-5. Record the specific words Paul used to describe the condition of humanity apart from Christ.

Do you think most people view their condition as this desperate? Why or why not?

Despite what modern psychological mumbo jumbo will tell you, we're not all OK. We're not even a little OK. According to the Bible, we're dead. Now let's be clear on this point, because a dead person doesn't need help. Nor does he need a shove in the right direction. A dead person needs something miraculous.

The dead need an outside force to act on them because their condition is one of complete and total helplessness. They can only be manipulated; they don't have the capability of doing a single thing in and of themselves. This is the truth of our condition, and thank God that He loves us enough to tell us the truth.

We might coddle one another with platitudes and sentiments, but if we could really see our inner condition, we would know our deadness doesn't only mean we aren't good enough to go to heaven. It also means we are joyfully headed to hell.

Read Romans 5:1. If the gospel brings peace with God, then what is our relationship with God when we are separated from the gospel?

How did you recognize that you needed to be saved?

We are rebels against God, and we love it. We need His grace not only to save us but also to open our eyes to the very fact that we need saving. The tragic nature of our condition is that we are bloated corpses, floating in the sea of sin, all the while telling one another we're OK.

God help us.

PRAY TODAY FOR A GREATER SENSE OF WHAT YOU HAVE BEEN SAVED FROM. REJOICE IN THE GOOD NEWS OF THE GOSPEL, THROUGH WHICH YOU WERE NOT ONLY SAVED BUT ALSO BECAME AWARE OF YOUR NEED TO BE SAVED.

The Gospel Makes You Holy

It is only by the gracious work of God that we become aware of our great need. And it's only by the gracious work of God that we can be made alive again in Christ. The gospel miraculously saves us and changes us from traitors to children, from enemies to beloved sons and daughters. But the good news doesn't stop there.

Read Romans 8:28-30. Which part of this passage do you think Christians are more likely to focus on? Why?

What implications do verses 29-30 have for verse 28?

Romans 8:28 is one of those well-worn Bible passages that most people know by heart. Like John 3:16, it's one we pull out from our back pocket when the situation demands it and slap it down on hurting people to tell them everything will be OK.

But this verse must be understood within the context of the paragraph. And that paragraph must be understood within the context of the entire book. And that book must be understood within the context of the entire Bible.

So you can't have Romans 8:28 without verses 29-30, and those verses remind us what *good* really is and define God's purpose that we have been called to. Namely, it's that we would be conformed to the image of Jesus Christ.

In your own words, what does it mean to be conformed to the image of Jesus Christ?

How have you seen God work out this purpose in your life?

Regardless of who you are, where you're from, or what baggage you bring to the gospel, your destination is the same: to be like Jesus. The gospel not only saves us but also makes us holy. By God's grace we were justified. By God's grace we will be sanctified or conformed to Jesus' likeness. And by God's grace we will eventually be glorified.

Often, though, it's while trying to grow in holiness that we start to focus less and less on the gospel and more and more on our own work.

Do agree that most of our growth in holiness focuses on our work rather than the gospel? Why?

Is it easier or harder to grow in grace-driven holiness rather than works-driven holiness?

If both methods grow us in holiness, does it matter how the holiness is attained?

The last question in the previous activity is particularly important at this stage. The means by which we grow really matters. Look back at Romans 8:29-30. Do you see who is doing all the work in these verses? It's God. It's God who predestines. It's God who calls. It's God who justifies. And it's God who glorifies. We are the objects, the ones being changed. Because growing in holiness is all God's work in our lives, we have only one option at the end of that process: to give God the glory He deserves.

Growth in holiness that is driven by our effort rather than God's grace is really a sly attempt by our idolatrous hearts to steal and claim credit for what rightfully belongs to God. If we grew because of our strong effort and moral fortitude, we would justly share in the glory of God. But God isn't willing to share His glory.

Additionally, when it comes to being holy, it's quite a stretch to think we can actually do this. We've got a long way to go to be conformed to the image of Jesus. If we rely on our own strength, that strength is going to run out long before we get to the goal.

The glorious truth is that we are made holy the same way we were saved from hell: through the inexhaustible grace of God. Only by trusting in His power rather than our own can we glory in Him and move forward in our pursuit of Christlikeness.

Are you trusting in your own strength or in the grace of God in your pursuit of holiness?

PRAY TODAY, EXPRESSING YOUR FAITH AND CONFIDENCE IN GOD'S ABILITY TO MAKE YOU HOLY. CONFESS THAT YOU BELIEVE ALL THINGS ARE WORKING TOWARD THAT END—FOR YOUR GOOD AND FOR HIS PURPOSE.

The Gospel Sustains You

The gospel saves you. The gospel makes you holy. And the gospel will keep you to the end. This is another element of the gospel that is often overlooked because most of us can't foresee a day when we would stop believing the truths of Jesus' life, death, and resurrection. But scores of people have gone before us with the very same intention.

What kinds of things in life might make someone abandon their supposed belief in the gospel?

What makes you sure you never would?

To begin with, let's be realistic about what we believe. It's a centuries-old story about a man who lived a perfect life. Not only that, but He had perfect intentions that drove every one of His actions. Anyone who has ever seen the blackness and duplicity of their own heart realizes the impossibility of that statement.

But it gets more absurd. This man was tried and convicted as a criminal and was put to death in the most humiliating, painful way ever devised. During this torture He actually prayed for the souls of those spitting in His face.

Jesus died and was buried. Case closed. Except after three days He rose from the dead and appeared to more than five hundred people (see 1 Cor. 15:6). The whole thing is preposterous. It's lunacy. It's an absolute contradiction of the laws of physics, as well as human nature. Yet this is what Christ followers stake our whole lives on.

How did Paul describe the message of the gospel in 1 Corinthians 1:18-25?

No wonder Paul called the message of the cross foolishness (see 1 Cor. 1:18). It certainly is that. But the intrinsic craziness of the message isn't the only reason we can't put our faith in our own ability to continue believing.

Read Matthew 13:1-8,18-23. Which of the people described in this parable were truly Christians? How do you know?

Jesus wasn't willing to pull any punches in His teaching. He always called it the way He saw it and was willing to tell people the truth even when it was hard to accept. In this parable, for example, the people described in verse 19 were obviously not Christians. They didn't seem to believe the gospel, even at first hearing. But after that the situation becomes a bit more complicated.

In verse 20 the person heard the word of the kingdom of God and received it with joy. But then because of external pressure, hardship, or persecution, he decided that this whole Jesus thing wasn't really for him after all. In verse 22 something similar happened, but the abandonment came as a result of loving the material things of the world. In each of these cases, the people had no intent of leaving the faith. But they did.

We can't trust in our own strength to believe the gospel. We will fall short. There will be days when we don't feel like believing. There will be times of great sadness and loss when it doesn't seem as if anything we believe is real. So what will we do then? What will we count on when our strength and will are gone?

Recall a time when you were discouraged or doubtful about your faith. What kinds of issues did you wrestle with?

What motivated you to keep believing during this period of your life?

The great news of the gospel is that we aren't trusting in our own strength to persevere in faith. We are trusting in God's promise to uphold us.

Read Philippians 1:1-6. How did Paul feel about the Philippian church?

How confident was Paul about their perseverance in faith? How do you know?

The apostle had a very close relationship with this group of believers. In this passage he called them his partners in the gospel, and he meant that literally. The people of this church, for example, were some of the few from whom Paul was willing to accept financial support. He denied others that privilege in order to avoid any charge of greed or favoritism. But he felt strongly enough about the faith and intentions of the Philippians that he counted them as his close friends in Christ. Yet even in the case of the Philippians, for whom he always thanked God every time he remembered them (see v. 3), Paul had confidence in God rather than in them.

That's what verse 6 tells us. Paul's confidence was not in the Philippians' ability to remain true to the gospel; it was in the fact that God is able to sustain the faith of everyone who truly believes in the gospel.

No matter what life throws at you, no matter what the circumstance or temptation is, you can be confident moving forward in faith. But it's not because you believe so strongly. It's because in the gospel, God will finish the work He started in you.

PRAY IN THANKSGIVING TODAY FOR GOD'S POWER TO UPHOLD YOUR FAITH. EXPRESS CONFIDENCE THAT HE WILL ENABLE YOU TO CONTINUE TO BELIEVE, NO MATTER WHAT YOUR LIFE CIRCUMSTANCES MIGHT BE.

The Gospel for Life

As we close this week, let's return to 1 Corinthians 15. This chapter contains one of the most succinct yet most comprehensive and clear articulations of the gospel in the Bible. This was the entire summation of Paul's message in town after town as he proclaimed the good news.

But the key for us to notice at this point is so simple that it can almost escape our notice: this passage was written to a church. *To Christians.*

Why would Paul preach the gospel to Christians—those who have already believed the gospel?

Is there a principle there for us in the church today? Why might we need to hear the gospel over and over again?

Read 1 Corinthians 2:1-5. What do you think Paul meant when he wrote that he "didn't think it was a good idea to know anything among you except Jesus Christ and Him crucified" (v. 2)?

Why, according to verse 5, was Paul not concerned with using wise and persuasive words?

You could argue from this passage that Paul wasn't very seeker-sensitive. He didn't have any clever illustrations or an incredible band backing him up. All he was armed with was the message of Jesus' bloody death and beautiful resurrection. But in his mind that was more than enough, not only to enter life with Christ but also to sustain those who did.

There is a phenomenon in modern Christianity that would be very foreign to someone like Paul. It's the thinking that the gospel is the beginning of the Christian experience, something that's no doubt very important but something that only launches us into the real business of living the Christian life. We are supposed to understand the gospel initially but then move past it to the deeper things of faith.

What? Nowhere in the Bible do you find this mentality. Nowhere do you find people moving past the gospel like it's merely the starting point.

Instead, you find again and again the truth that the gospel is for all of life. The truth of Jesus' life, death, and resurrection has such profound implications that it changes our perspective, approach, and dealings in everything we do, from the way we eat our food to the way we deal with cancer.

Look back at 1 Corinthians 15:1-8. Where do you see Paul emphasizing that the gospel is for all of life rather than only the beginning point of Christianity?

Do you agree that Christians seem eager to move past the gospel? If so, why do you think that's the case?

Think about a gospel-centered life. What attributes do you think would characterize the life of someone who dwells on the gospel every day?

Having trouble with your children? Preach the gospel to them and to yourself. Frustrated with your boss? Remember the gospel. Having trouble controlling your emotions? Think about the gospel. Wondering what to study in college? Dwell on the gospel.

The gospel is for all of life. When we think of the gospel as applying only to a specific experience, we aren't embracing the fullness of what Jesus did on our behalf.

Record any areas of your life in which you are leaving the gospel out of the picture. What difference would it make if you applied the truth and power of the gospel to these situations, problems, or relationships?

The gospel is such a transformational message that it leaves no stone unturned, no corner of our lives unreached. Again and again Scripture emphasizes that what we need more than anything else in life is the gospel. The rest of this study will help us see how the explicit gospel comes to bear on every part of our existence.

When you start to see the gospel in that light, you begin to understand that it's not just the starting point. Growing deeper in Christ isn't moving past the gospel; it's moving further into it. And what we'll find is that no matter how deep we go, there is still more to explore.

PRAY TODAY THAT GOD WILL OPEN YOUR EYES FURTHER AND FURTHER TO THE GREATNESS AND SUFFICIENCY OF THE GOSPEL.

Week 2
The Gospel
Saves You

Start

Welcome back to this small-group discussion of *The Explicit Gospel.*

What struck you as new or interesting in week 1 of the workbook?

Take a few minutes to discuss the gospel's role in salvation. What are we saved from? How is salvation possible? How do we access salvation?

How can we tell whether our growth in holiness is founded on God's grace (the gospel) or on our own efforts? What are the symptoms of both?

At the end of the previous group experience, you identified one action you could take to gain a better understanding and practice of the gospel. If you are comfortable doing so, share whether you were able to take that action and anything you experienced as a result.

To prepare to view the DVD segment, read aloud Psalm 19:7-10:

> *The instruction of the Lord is perfect,*
> *renewing one's life;*
> *the testimony of the Lord is trustworthy,*
> *making the inexperienced wise.*
> *The precepts of the Lord are right,*
> *making the heart glad;*
> *the command of the Lord is radiant,*
> *making the eyes light up.*
> *The fear of the Lord is pure,*
> *enduring forever;*
> *the ordinances of the Lord are reliable*
> *and altogether righteous.*
> *They are more desirable than gold—*
> *than an abundance of pure gold;*
> *and sweeter than honey,*
> *which comes from the honeycomb.*

Watch

Complete the viewer guide below as you view DVD session 2.

All of the ills that befall mankind are symptoms of a greater _____.

All human beings are guilty of three things:

   1. All of us prefer _____ to the Creator.

   2. We think we're _____ than God.

   3. We've all failed to _____ Him.

If you could _____ yourself, you would still be guilty of failing to acknowledge _____.

You are in desperate need of someone who does not _____, to _____.

Through the law no one will stand _____ before God.

You went from having no righteousness of your own to getting the righteousness of _____ Himself.

You didn't justify _____. You were justified.

You are, without any ability to argue your cause, _____.

We have lost a _____ of God.

We will give an _____ to God.

It's a righteousness that is given to you in _____ _____.

Video sessions available for purchase at *lifeway.com/explicitgospel*

Respond

Discuss the DVD segment with your group, using the questions below.

What did you like best about the DVD segment? Why?

Matt identified three things that are ultimately wrong with us as human beings: We prefer creation to the Creator, we believe we're smarter than God, and we fail to acknowledge Him. Which of these flaws is most prevalent in today's culture? Which has affected your life the most?

What does it mean to have a healthy fear of God?

What step can you take this week to let go of your self-righteousness and take hold of the true righteousness that has been offered to you by Christ? Again, if you're comfortable, share this step with the group.

Conclude the group discussion with a time of prayer and confession before God. Whether you prefer to pray silently or aloud, speak with God about your flaws: the ways you've valued creation over Him, believed yourself to be smarter than He, and failed to acknowledge Him. Ask God to grant you a healthy fear of Him along with the righteousness He's already offered.

Suggested Scripture memory for this week: ROMANS 3:20
No one will be justified in His sight by the works of the law, because the knowledge of sin comes through the law.

Read week 2 and complete the activities before the next group experience.

Was Jesus serious when He warned people about hell?

As you scan the Gospel records of Jesus' teachings on hell, you come to understand that it's nothing to be played around with.

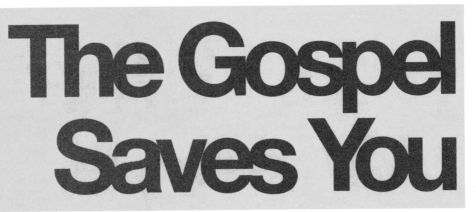

The Gospel Saves You

When Jesus spoke about eternity, He was dead serious, unwilling to pull any punches. You get images of worms that never die and fiery retribution that goes on eternally. Jesus wasn't interested in playing down the horrible truth.

But in our day, when most Christians (at least in North America) have never been in want for anything and rarely have bigger dilemmas than weight gain after the holidays or a downturn in a prosperous economy, such language comes across as extreme. Or maybe at least a little mean.

Our failure to realize the gravity of eternity reveals several issues at play in our lives. An underestimation of the nature of sin. An overestimation of our own abilities. And a drastic downplay of the extremity of God's grace.

Because we don't take eternity as seriously as Jesus did, we must return to the core of the explicit gospel, realizing once again that the gospel indeed saves us. And we desperately need saving.

What's Wrong with the World?

Take a look around the world. Sure, there's beauty, but there's also tragedy at every turn. We all recognize that things go wrong in the world of nature. We are firsthand observers of disasters like hurricanes, blizzards, tornadoes, tsunamis, and volcanic eruptions. Those things are bad.

Typically, though, we don't think of these events as anyone's fault. Insurance adjusters classify them as acts of God because the fault can't be assigned to anyone else. And although an earthquake doesn't happen because you stole a piece of candy from the convenience store, there is blame to be assigned. These acts of nature point us to something bigger than ourselves—and to the fact that the world as we know it is broken.

Read Romans 8:18-24. What are some terms Paul used to describe the state of creation?

What, then, is the ultimate cause of all these disasters?

Paul wrote that creation is eagerly longing for something; it desires something. Creation has been subjected to futility, which means creation has been knocked down from where it *was* to where it *is*. Further, Paul described this longing and groaning as something like childbirth.

The world is in pain. So not only do the mountains sing and trees clap (see Isa. 55:12), rocks cry (see Luke 19:40) and heavens declare (see Ps. 19:1). Creation also longs and groans for release. In fact, the natural order of the universe is reacting to the introduction of sin into its midst. If we go back to the very beginning of the story, we know it hasn't always been like this.

Read Genesis 1:1,10,12,18,21,25,31. What refrain is repeated in these verses?

What does the Bible mean when it says, "It was good"?

Sometimes we sell the creative capacity of God short. We acknowledge that He created physical objects like a rock and a tree. But let's not stop there. The classic phrase used to describe God's activity is ex nihilo; that is, He created something from nothing. It's not as if God had a lump of clay and formed it into something else. There was nothing—and then there was everything. And everything is pretty far-reaching.

The color pink? God's idea. The taste of an avocado? That was God. Feelings and emotions? God. Everything finds its source in God, and every aspect of creation, from the largest galaxy to the tiniest burst of flavor in seasoning, radiates the goodness of God.

How might you honor God's creative capacity today through an everyday activity you take for granted?

In its rightful order the world was made for God's glory. But when sin entered us, it entered the world. Original sin has effects beyond humanity; it affects the world, the cosmos. Rebellion against God disrupts the order of everything.

Read Genesis 3:17-19. What far-reaching implications of sin do you see in this passage?

What, then, is the reason behind natural disasters like tsunamis and blizzards?

The harmony Adam and Eve enjoyed with God's creation, the peaceful dominion they were given over it, was broken when they ate a piece of forbidden fruit. Adam and Eve were placed as the crowns of God's good creation, but as the crown goes, so goes creation. Their sin brought a curse to us all, and the curse is found as far as the east is from the west.

Work was accomplished without toil; now it's toilsome. The earth was readily subdued; now it yields grudgingly. Adam was bestowed with imperishable flesh; now his sin limits the lifespan of the body.

It would be great to live in Genesis 1–2. There's no subjection to futility there, no bondage to corruption, no slavery to death. That would be a dream, but it's not the world we live in. It's not where our children grow up, it's not where we work, and it's not where we live. Here, now, things have gone haywire.

What physical evidence of a broken world have you encountered this week?

Are you starting to get the picture? The gospel is about God's making all things new, not just in us but in the entire universe. Because of the great harm sin has wrought on all creation, the only solution is something even greater—something on a cosmic scale.

Enter the gospel.

PRAY TODAY FOR THOSE AROUND YOU WHO ARE EXPERIENCING THE EFFECTS OF A BROKEN WORLD. PRAY THAT THEY WILL PUT THEIR FULL HOPE AND FAITH IN THE GOSPEL.

What's Wrong with Me?

In Genesis 3 we observe the tragic fracturing of the universe. Everything was affected, from the attitude of the rabbit to the sinful nature of humanity. Just as hurricanes ravage islands in the sea, sin tears apart the human heart. We can look at the world around us and acknowledge it's badly broken, and we can turn our eyes inward and see the devastation of sin in our lives.

Do you think Christians take sin seriously enough? Why or why not?

If you boiled it down to one thing, what is the root of sin?

Sin came into the cosmos through the garden, but that's not the real root. The root of sin lies in the very reason we were created to begin with and our betrayal of that purpose. We are, by nature, a worshiping people. We only have to look around our culture to see proof of this.

Grown men paint their bodies and surf an incalculable number of Web sites to follow a sports team. People spontaneously lift their hands and clap and close their eyes at concerts. We put posters on our walls, stickers on our cars, and ink on our skin. All of this provides evidence that we are hardwired for worship. It's an innate desire, an instinctive impulse in our DNA, given to us as a gift from God.

What are some other practices you've observed that point to our innate desire to worship something?

Why would worship, when directed at God, be a gift from Him to His creation?

Some find it troubling to think God created humanity to worship Him. It sounds selfish and egotistical of God, but that's only because we are viewing Him through the lens of human experience. When someone in our lives constantly demands our attention and focus, it's vanity. But it's also deception, because no person deserves that amount of attention.

But God does. As the embodiment of everything good and right and true, He alone deserves the praise of the universe. Furthermore, it's only through worshiping Him alone that we can truly find joy and satisfaction. If that's the case, not only is it right for God to command us to worship Him, but it's also loving. If He failed to do so, He would be withholding His greatest gift from humanity—Himself.

But what happens when instead of using the gift of worship from God *for* God, we invest our worship in the stuff God made? What happens when we attempt to hijack God's story about Himself and rewrite it with ourselves at the center? Just take a look around. That's what happens.

Recall the account of Adam and Eve's sin in Genesis 3. Where do you see worship in this story?

How did their decision betray the worship of God?

When Adam and Eve chose to eat the forbidden fruit, they committed insurrection. Infernal mutiny. Though they had an infinitely valuable, infinitely deep, infinitely rich, infinitely wise, infinitely loving God, they chose a piece of fruit. Rather than pursuing Him with steadfast passion and enthralled fury; instead of loving Him with all their heart, soul, mind, and strength; instead of attributing to Him glory and honor and praise and power and wisdom and strength, they wanted a snack.

That should sound familiar because we do the same thing every day. What in the world is wrong with us?

Read Paul's description of sin in Romans 1:18-25. Which part of this passage is the most vivid to you?

Where specifically do you see the link to worship in this passage?

How does this passage speak broadly to the human condition of sinfulness?

How does this passage remind you of a way you have chosen to worship something besides God?

Reading Paul's description, you begin to see the lunacy of sin. When our paltry pleasures are stacked up against an infinite God, the choosing of the former can be nothing less than craziness. And yet that's what we do over and over again. Because we do, we should be very careful to do what Paul advocates in Romans 11:22: "Consider God's kindness and severity."

TODAY TAKE PAUL'S ADVICE. IN PRAYER CONSIDER GOD'S SEVERITY IN LIGHT OF YOUR OWN REBELLION.

It Really Is That Bad

Paul said to note God's severity (see Rom. 11:22). Mark it down. Remember it. Consider it. But we are disobedient at every turn. Because God's severity isn't as warm and fuzzy as God's kindness, we not only fail to study or contemplate it but also refuse to note it.

Why would Paul direct us to consider the severity of God?

What three words immediately come to mind when you consider God's severity?

1.

2.

3.

Read Jeremiah 2:11-12. What did God command the universe to do when His people embraced idolatry?

Make no mistake: whether or not we consider it, God is severe. And the betrayal of His glory is a severe action. That's why in Jeremiah 2 God commanded the universe to shudder in terror at the idea of idolatry.

Jesus certainly considered God's severity, and He called others to do the same. Jesus used the word *gehenna* 12 times in the four Gospels. We would translate the word *hell*. It probably refers to a ravine on the south side of Jerusalem where, about a hundred years before Jesus was born, odd murders were going on. The Jews began to view this area as cursed. It became a trash heap or dumping ground for the city. When the pile got too big, the whole thing was set on fire.

Can you picture this? The word *gehenna* conjures up a very vivid image: a stinking, smoldering place of destruction and neglect.

Why would Jesus have chosen this trash dump as an image of hell?

What emotion was He trying to inspire in His audience?

When Jesus talked about hell this way, He wanted people to have a mental image of hell that is putrid and repulsive; it's dead and deadly; it's smoldering when not blazing. It's utterly desolate, spiritually dark, and endlessly oppressive.

It's at this point that our sensibilities start to get offended. Maybe the internal monologue sounds something like this: *I know sin is a big deal, but is it that big? Really? It's not as though I've killed anybody. I can understand a fate like that is fitting for some people but not for me.*

What are the underlying assumptions of that line of thinking?

Why is hell indeed that bad?

In your heart do you really believe you deserve that?

I hope you're beginning to see some of the assumptions that prop up our objections to hell. We don't really think we're that bad. And we don't think we're that bad because we don't think our sin is really that bad.

But the solution isn't to think about our sin. That's how we got into this problem in the first place. If all we ever do is think about our sin, we're still living in a state of self-worship. We can really begin to see the awful nature of sin only when we behold the wonderful goodness of God.

Because we're so self-centered, we find it difficult, even for a moment, to pry our eyes away from our beloved selves, even if we're thinking about how bad our sin is. But if we could, we'd see the glory and beauty of the Lord. And in response, we'd be absolutely terrified.

Read Romans 3:19. In your own words, what does it mean that "every mouth may be shut"?

We might offer up our good works right now, along with our excuses for our sin, but in the end every mouth will be closed. When we all behold God as He truly is, there will be no doubt about what we truly deserve.

We deserve the worst because God is the best. Sin really is that bad because God is simply that good.

ACKNOWLEDGE YOUR SIN AS HONESTLY AS YOU CAN BEFORE GOD TODAY. OFFER NO EXCUSES AS YOU CONSIDER HIS SEVERITY.

The Wisdom of God in the Cross

Paul admonished us, "Consider God's kindness and severity: severity toward those who have fallen but God's kindness toward you" (Rom. 11:22). The severity of God is justified. And it's terrifying. But the truth is that we can consider the magnitude of God's kindness only when we also consider His severity.

Reread the previous statement. How can considering God's severity lead us to truly consider His kindness?

How would our consideration of God's kindness be affected if we didn't also consider His severity?

Considering God's severity is good and right. It's good information to know. But it's not sufficient to move us to praise God. Knowledge of hell alone is unable to create worshipers. Contrary to what we might think (and even practice in many cases), we can't scare the hell out of someone. We can scare people into coming to church, trying to be good, giving money, and even walking an aisle and praying a certain prayer, but we can't scare people into loving God.

To highlight only the breadth of the chasm is not to bridge it. So why highlight it at all? Because we can't understand the cross of Christ without understanding the weight of the glory of God, the offense of belittling His name, and the just punishment for that offense. What Christ did on the cross will not produce transforming love until we see that the cross also reveals the depth of the offense of sin.

Enter grace. And consider the kindness of God.

Why do you think Jesus had to die for the sins of humankind?

Read Romans 6:23. In using the word *wages,* what did Paul imply about the nature of the punishment for sin?

God's innate righteousness demands justice. He can't let guilt go unpunished. Because the transgression is so grievous, the payment must equal the measure of the sin.

Read Hebrews 9:22. Why do you think without blood there is no remission of sin?

Where do you see the principle of Hebrews 9:22 in action in the Old Testament?

Throughout the Old Testament, blood was always flowing. Abel, Noah, Abraham, Isaac, and Jacob all worshiped God through blood sacrifices. Then, after the Israelites entered the promised land, blood constantly flowed from the temple. Can you imagine the stench in Jerusalem? Can you imagine hundreds and thousands of people regularly carrying goats, lambs, chickens, or doves into the place of sacrifice; cutting their throats; and draining their blood?

Sounds pretty violent, right? It's supposed to. The blood reminds us of the severity of sin. Sin results in death. But the fact that the blood was flowing from sacrifices rather than from sinners themselves makes us consider the kindness of God. He loves His children and is therefore patient with them, wanting them all to come to repentance. We deserve His wrath, but He refuses to give us what we deserve.

Did those Old Testament sacrifices really remove the sin of God's people?

If not, why did God command such a system to be practiced for hundreds of years?

Let's be honest. Do we really think the blood of a goat can be enough to pay for sin, in light of God's severity? *It's a goat!* The writer of Hebrews said, "It is impossible for the blood of bulls and goats to take away sins" (Heb. 10:4). No, all of those sacrifices pointed to the one single sacrifice that would satisfy the wrath and justice of God.

How do people without Christ try to deal with their sin?

Have you ever responded to guilt in your life without taking it to Jesus? What was the result?

Read Romans 3:23-26. From God's perspective, what did the cross do?

The gospel holds out for us a place where God's kindness and severity meet, where grace and wrath intersect. This place is called the cross. We can stand back and marvel at the wisdom of God, for it's at the cross where God in His wisdom provided a way for love and justice to meet each other ... and kiss.

We like to think love wins out at the cross, and in a sense it does. But love doesn't win at the expense of justice. Rather, the cross shows us both the uncompromising love and the uncompromising justice of God. It showcases the awful severity of God as the just wrath of the Almighty was poured out on His Son. The cross showcases the beautiful kindness of God as His wondrous love releases sinners from their bondage and guilt through the substitutionary sacrifice of Jesus.

The cross changes everything.

TODAY THANK GOD FOR THE CROSS. THANK HIM FOR SATISFYING HIS OWN WRATH AND IN HIS LOVE PROVIDING FORGIVENESS FOR YOUR SIN.

A Whole Life

The cross changes everything. The cross satisfies the justified wrath of God, and God Himself is the justifier. On the other side of Calvary—and only then–can we live with purpose and meaning. Apart from the cross our lives are utterly and hopelessly lost. Completely meaningless.

Read Ecclesiastes 1:1-2 in as many versions of the Bible as you can. What are some words from those different versions that the Teacher used to describe life?

Why do you think this man described life as "absolute futility" (v. 2)?

Ecclesiastes 1:1 tells us this book contains "the words of the Teacher." Right out of the gate we learn that this is more than just a life story; it is the chronicle of a lesson learned. The author was Solomon, the king of a prosperous, wealthy, powerful nation. He had more wealth, power, and fame than you'll ever have. And yet he described life as absolute futility.

The word *futility* in Hebrew conveys a sense of meaningless. Chipper introduction, huh? Now we can all look at life and agree that some parts have no purpose—like neckties and cats. But Solomon took it a step further to say *everything* in life is meaningless.

Marriage? Pleasure? Wealth? Education? All meaningless. Methodically over the course of 12 chapters he wrote about every aspect of living and then attached worthlessness to it. He used the Hebrew word *hebel* 38 times before he was done.

Have you ever felt that life had no meaning? What were your circumstances?

Why do you think you felt that way?

Read Ecclesiastes 1:4-7. In your own words, how was Solomon describing life?

Solomon described life as if it's a treadmill. We get caught up in this silly circular pattern, and each generation runs with all the vigor of the sweaty guy on the treadmill at the gym. And when all is said and done, we don't go anywhere.

Don't fool yourself. Until we honestly evaluate this life under the sun, until we are ready to look at our lives and see that real meaning lies outside the world's system, we will be stuck on the treadmill. This place is broken. There's no sense in looking to the world for the fix.

The Bible, however, offers a solution. The word the Bible uses for the opposite of this condition is *shalom*. It means *wholeness*.

Why is wholeness the opposite of the life Solomon described?

Where do you most sense the lack of wholeness in your life?

The gospel is the message of wholeness. It's what Jesus brings to us, thanks to the cross. And one of the most vivid accounts of this is found in John 4. Jesus decided to go through Samaria despite the fact that nobody went there, especially not Jews. He sat down at a well, and a woman who was exchanging sex for rent showed up. She came to the well in the middle of the day because if she had gone in the morning, she probably would have been beaten up. She was a complete outcast.

What ensued was an exchange about water. Jesus, in essence, asked the woman if she was tired of the treadmill. Every day going back and forth for water, then doing it again.

Read John 4:10-14. How do Jesus' words counter Solomon's words from Ecclesiastes?

The woman completely missed the point. She said, "You don't even have a cup. What are You talking about?"

What was Jesus talking about? He was saying, "I am eternal. I fill the void. I fit the groove." Whether or not we realize it, we're all looking for shalom—real wholeness. In the end nothing under the sun brings lasting fulfillment. We have to look beyond the sun. The groove in our hearts can't be filled with the temporal. It demands eternity. Therefore, our very searching for more and more, for bigger and bigger, for better and better is our sense that something is off, amiss, deformed, and broken in our souls. Only Jesus makes us whole. In Him we have shalom.

PRAY TODAY, EMBRACING THE WHOLENESS JESUS BRINGS. ASK GOD TO WEAN YOU OFF THE TEMPORAL IN ORDER TO EMBRACE THE ETERNAL.

Week 3
The Gospel Matures You

Start

Welcome back to this small-group discussion of *The Explicit Gospel*.

At the end of the previous group experience, you identified one step you could take to let go of self-righteousness and embrace the righteousness offered by Christ. If you are comfortable, share whether you were able to take that step and what you experienced as a result.

What struck you as new or interesting in week 2 of the workbook?

Jesus mentioned hell several times in the Gospels. What other passages of Scripture refer to hell, and what can we learn from them?

How have you personally experienced God's severity? His kindness?

To prepare to view the DVD segment, read aloud Colossians 1:15-20.

He is the image of the invisible God,
the firstborn over all creation.
For everything was created by Him,
in heaven and on earth,
the visible and the invisible,
whether thrones or dominions
or rulers or authorities—
all things have been created through Him and for Him.
He is before all things,
and by Him all things hold together.
He is also the head of the body, the church;
He is the beginning, the firstborn from the dead,
so that He might come to have
first place in everything.
For God was pleased to have
all His fullness dwell in Him,
and through Him to reconcile everything to Himself
by making peace through the blood of His cross—
whether things on earth or things in heaven.

Watch

Complete the viewer guide below as you view DVD session 3.

The gospel pushes us toward _____ and _____.

We can't talk about holiness and righteousness that are rooted in joy if you're not a _____.

Is there an internal desire and delight in you for _____?

We've got no shot at holiness and righteousness if we haven't been _____ _____.

To grow in holiness, you set your eyes, your mind, and your heart on _____.

To be conformed to a pattern of _____ is not the same thing as being _____ by the Holy Spirit of God.

If intimacy with God, for you, hinges on your ability to manage your _____, you will never walk intimately with God.

The more you pursue Christ and know Him, the more you're transformed into His _____.

Sin loses its _____ on our hearts when God is a greater _____ than the things below.

Actively do two things:
1. Actively grow in _____ of Jesus Christ and filling our lives with things that help that delight.
2. Put to death that which is _____.

If this is where the Enemy is going to get you and the flesh is going to draw you somewhere, act _____ against those things.

Video sessions available for purchase at *lifeway.com/explicitgospel*

Respond

Discuss the DVD segment with your group, using the questions below.

What emotions did you experience while watching the DVD segment? Why?

In your own words, talk about what it means to be a Christian. What does it look like to live as a Christian?

Drawing from the DVD segment and your own experiences, what practical steps can Christians take to set their eyes, minds, and hearts on Christ?

Which of those practical steps are you willing to take this week in order to grow in holiness? For increased accountability, consider sharing this step with the rest of the group.

Matt said, "With our minds set on that which is above, it becomes easy to put to death that which is below." Do you agree with that principle? Why or why not?

What actions or activities stir your affections toward Christ? Take one minute to write below some of those actions or activities.

Take another minute to write what prevents you from experiencing those actions or activities more often.

Suggested Scripture memory for this week: COLOSSIANS 3:2-3
Set your minds on what is above, not on what is on the earth. For you have died, and your life is hidden with the Messiah in God.

Read week 3 and complete the activities before the next group experience.

Isn't the gospel all about salvation?

The gospel includes salvation. But it's more than fire insurance.

The Gospel Matures You

Most of us can recite the facts of the gospel. Born in a manger, shepherds and wise men, perfect life, lots of healing, death on a cross, resurrection. Is that everything?

And when we're pressed to talk about what these facts mean for us, the standard answer is heaven. Thanks to Jesus, we get to go to heaven. That's true enough, but it's radically incomplete. In fact, there are pews full of people who are practically just waiting to die. That's what their faith is all about—making sure they don't burn.

In the worst cases this fire-insurance mentality creates laziness in supposed believers. They've got the end taken care of, so the way they live doesn't matter much. But a true understanding, love, and embracing of the gospel not only secure us in this life but also move us to action in this life.

The gospel makes us mature.

New Creations

What comes to your mind when you think about growing in Christ? Education classes? Spiritual discipline? Crucifying the flesh? Those things are good and right. As Christians, we're meant to grow in love, discipline, knowledge, and holiness. That's what it means to mature. But the attitude with which we approach this spiritual growth is critically important.

Most people tend to err in one of two ways. First, many think salvation is about God's work in Christ, but spiritual growth and maturity are about your work. You work hard at praying, reading the Bible, fasting, and church attendance. The extent to which you mature in your faith rests squarely on your shoulders and is achieved by the sweat of your brow.

The other extreme is to look at growth in Christ as an optional supplement to the Christian life. You've got that heaven-or-hell issue covered, and everything else is gravy, so you sit back and wait, maybe picking up a fact or two from a sermon every now and then.

Do you see yourself in either of these two errors?

What is wrong with each one?

How might spiritual growth in maturity be linked to the gospel?

In our minds there's a separation between the gospel and spiritual growth. We think the gospel starts the process, but the rest is up to us. When we take that view, we show that we don't really have a full understanding of what happens to us in the gospel. Thanks to Jesus' life, death, and resurrection, we have become completely new people with a new purpose. Our destiny is to pursue that purpose, driven on by the power of the gospel.

Read Matthew 22:34-40. What was the intent of the Pharisee's question?

According to Jesus, how important was His answer?

Does Jesus' command bother you? Why or why not?

The excruciatingly difficult thing about Jesus' response to this Pharisee was not its importance. We can see that everything in the law of God hinges on love for Him and for our neighbor. The first four Commandments are about love for God, and the second six are about love for others. All of the other laws are built on the fact that if you really love God with every part of your being, the rest of the law will take care of itself.

The hard part is that the command Jesus gave is absolutely, unequivocally impossible.

Why is Jesus' command to love God impossible?

You can force yourself to submit to someone. But you can't force yourself to love someone. Even as you tried to obey that command, there would be an element of resentment in your heart. You would obey because you had to—out of fear, obligation, or guilt. That's not love.

This is where the gospel goes deeper, because Jesus knows in our brokenness we don't have the capacity to love God. In order to carry out Jesus' command, we don't just need help; we need to be made into new people.

Read the way Paul described a believer's new identity in 2 Corinthians 5:15-21. What are some effects of this newness in Christ?

Do you get the significance of this? We are new creations in Christ. Brand-new. No wonder Jesus said faith in Him is the equivalent of being born again. But this time we aren't born with a sinful, twisted nature. We are born of the Spirit. Born to love God. Born to give our whole selves to Him and find in Him the fullness of joy. As new creations, we are wide awake to the wonders of God in the gospel.

Growing in Christ is the most natural thing in the world for a new creation to do. The gospel goes far beyond telling us good stuff to do; the gospel makes us into people who actually want to do those good things.

When you choose to sin as a new creation, you're going against the new nature God has secured inside you with the Holy Spirit. Conversely, when you choose godliness, righteousness, and holiness, you're embracing the good news of the change that has occurred in your life.

How does believing that you're a new creation alter the way you look at growing in Christ?

Growing in maturity in Christ is an expression of who you are. That's what the gospel does; it makes us new creations.

THANK GOD TODAY FOR YOUR NEW NATURE IN CHRIST. ASK HIM TO OPEN YOUR EYES TO SEE WHO YOU ARE IN JESUS.

A Violent Pursuit

You've been made new in Christ. That new identity incorporates new desires, new affections, and a new capacity to love and enjoy God. But if you've been a Christian for more than about five minutes, you also know the reality of the struggle inside you.

Read Galatians 5:16-17. What is the relationship between the flesh and the Spirit, according to these verses?

In what contexts have you felt the internal battle between the flesh and the Spirit?

If we're new creations in Christ, why do we still struggle with sin?

Anyone who has ever taken a serious look at the state of their heart and soul has felt the inner turmoil. Paul acknowledged this conflict in several passages, but the most explicit is Romans 7. As you scan this chapter, you can feel the anguish of the apostle as he ponders why he can't seem to quit doing what he doesn't want to do and why so often he can't seem to do what he wants to do.

No one who reads this chapter can say that pursuing holiness isn't hard work. We aren't idle spectators to the building of character and godliness in our lives.

Read the following passages. Note how each one expresses the effort involved in pursuing Christ and Christian living.

Romans 6:12-14

Romans 8:12-14

1 Corinthians 9:24-27

Philippians 3:12-14

Are you getting the theme? Run to win. Strain forward. Put to death the desires of the flesh. These aren't passive terms; they're active to the point of violence.

Paul didn't say to take your time in putting to death the desires of the flesh. Crucify them. Treat them with utter contempt and disavow them as violently as possible. This is the language of extreme effort. It's the power behind that effort, however, that's in question.

Read Romans 6:6-12. Notice the change in verb tense from verse 6 to verses 11-12. What does that change indicate to you?

Where does the power behind our effort come from?

In Romans 6:6 Paul wrote that our old self was crucified with Jesus so that sin's control over us would be abolished. That's past tense. We are new creations, and we are unbound from the yoke of sin. But Paul also said in verse 12 not to let sin reign in our mortal bodies. Even though we're new creations, the battle goes on inside us. On one side is the old sinful nature, which, though it does not have any lasting power over us, still hangs on with white knuckles. On the other side is the new self.

> The pursuit of holiness isn't a pursuit to become something different; it's the pursuit to live more and more like what we have already become. That's when this pursuit stops being the means to earn God's favor and starts being an expression of what God has done in us.

In the past has your pursuit of holiness been more about earning God's favor or recognizing what He's already done?

What will your attitude become if you pursue holiness as the means of earning God's favor? How is that different from the goal God has for you in Christ?

One pursuit is based on our effort. The other is based on God's work on our behalf. One puffs us up. The other makes us bow low. One results in our pride. The other results in worship, humility, and thankfulness. This is how the gospel moves us toward holiness. In the gospel we are reminded again and again of who we've become in Jesus.

That's powerful. It's transformational. And it's far better than just trying hard.

TODAY ASK GOD TO SEARCH YOUR HEART AND MOTIVES. ASK HIM TO SHOW YOU WHETHER YOU'RE PURSUING HOLINESS IN HIS POWER, STRENGTH, AND WORK OR AS A MEANS OF INFLATING YOURSELF.

Doing in Light of Done

People are going to respond to the gospel every time it's presented. They'll respond in belief, or their heart will become more and more hardened toward God. Make no mistake, though. This news demands a response.

So if we look at our lives today, a question we have to ask ourselves is this: *How am I responding to the good news of Jesus Christ? Am I stirred up toward obedience, or is Jesus becoming cliché to me? Am I becoming inoculated to Jesus, or do I find myself being more and more stirred to worship Him, to let other people know Him, and to submit my life fully to Him?*

Read 2 Corinthians 13:5. Why do you think Paul commands us to test ourselves?

What is the appropriate response to the gospel?

Let's be careful on this point. There are lots of ways we might respond to the previous question. Obedience. Worship. Joy. Evangelism. Absolutely but not primarily. The primary—and only—saving response to the gospel is faith. It must be from faith that all other responses flow.

Every good gift the Father gives—every rich treasure in Christ, every blessing from the Spirit—flows from the gospel and is received by faith.

Read the following passages. Beside each one, record what flows by faith.

Romans 3:22

Romans 11:29

Galatians 2:16

Galatians 3:26

Ephesians 3:17

Colossians 2:12

Hebrews 6:12

Hebrews 11:33

1 Peter 1:5

The list could go on and on. We live by faith, and we die by faith. Everything else is garbage. Even works of righteousness, if not done by faith, are works of self-righteousness and therefore filthy rags (see Phil. 3:8-9). Be careful about going to church, reading your Bible, saying prayers, doing good deeds, and reading books like this with any other motive than faith in the living Lord. The result of self-effort is belief in a phony Jesus and deadness to the gospel. Beware of just learning the jargon of Christianity and playing pretend in your Christian walk. Watch your life and your doctrine closely (see 1 Tim. 4:16). If you've become so good at being religious that you've deceived yourself, God help you.

We must make sure all of our doing is performed in light of done. We must make sure faith in Christ's finished work at the cross on our behalf is at the core of everything we do in life.

Read the way Paul described this dynamic in Colossians 3:1-5. What is the doing in this passage?

What is the done?

Do put to death what belongs in your worldly nature. Do pursue holiness. Do train yourself in godliness. Do live an upright, disciplined life. Do all of these things, but do them in light of what's done. When you're living in light of the cross, the gospel is never far from your mind.

The gospel motivates, empowers, and pushes you onward. Let's be honest: What alternatives to the cross are there? Be a good man? Be a good woman? Be a good Boy Scout or Girl Scout for Jesus? Not only is that foolishness; it's also utterly impossible. We'll run out of gas a mile into the trip.

Is anything you're doing motivated by a desire to get God's approval instead of a response to what He has done? How do you know?

There's a better way to live. It's the way to joyfully pursue holiness instead of grudgingly working for God. It's the way to humbly grow in righteousness instead of growing in pride. It's the way to know nothing "except Jesus Christ and Him crucified" (1 Cor. 2:2) in every aspect of life.

The good news is that you don't have to merit God's favor. He's already given it to you, thanks to Jesus. You can live in light of the finished work of the Son of God.

THANK GOD TODAY THAT YOU CAN LIVE IN LIGHT OF DONE. LET THE WORK HE HAS DONE THROUGH CHRIST FUEL YOU TO MOVE FORWARD IN GOOD WORKS.

The Weapons of Grace

The gospel of Jesus Christ—that God saves sinners through Jesus' perfect life, substitutionary death, and bodily resurrection—justifies us, but it also sanctifies us. *Justification* and *sanctification* are two vitally important words for Christians to understand. Justification is being right with God. Through Jesus' blood, sinners are welcomed into the presence of the holy King of the universe. Sanctification is the lifelong process that follows justification through which the Holy Spirit increasingly molds us into the likeness of Jesus.

The gospel is the extension of God's grace not only for justification but also for sanctification. What do we do, then, with all of God's commands in Scripture about our responsibility to pursue holiness, purity, and godly behavior? Let's be honest; the Bible is full of these. Put simply, we obey them. We try because if we don't, we will slip toward disobedience rather than obedience.

But to pursue holiness in the light of God's grace is radically different from trying to earn righteousness through our own effort. We must abandon the idea that there is any condemnation for those who are in Christ Jesus (see Rom. 8:1). We must reject the idea that our sins pile up on a scale that will earn God's punishment when tipped, as if Christ hadn't already taken this wrath for us on the cross.

Are you ever tempted to think bad things are happening to you because you are falling short in your Christian life?

How does that kind of thinking contradict the gospel?

We must also abandon the idea that our good behavior somehow rubs the spiritual lamp that inclines God, like a genie, to emerge and give us things we wish for.

Are you ever tempted to think you can merit God's blessings through your obedience?

How does this idea contradict the gospel?

When bad things happen—when we lose a job or get sick—we might attribute these things to ways we have failed God. And when good things happen, we sometimes think the business deal went through or the beloved said yes because we went on a mission trip or didn't miss a Sunday in church last year. But that's not how grace-driven effort works. Someone who understands the gospel and the cross instead fights sin with the weapons grace gives us. There are three such weapons.

The first weapon is the blood of Christ.

Read Ephesians 2:13. How does the way you deal with sin change when you understand that the blood of Christ has brought you near to God?

We have not been brought near to God by our behavior but by Jesus' sacrifice alone. The mark of believers who understand the gospel of Jesus Christ is that when they stumble and fall, when they make mistakes, they run to God and not from Him. They clearly understand that their acceptance by God is not predicated on their behavior but on the righteous life of Jesus Christ and His sacrificial death.

The second weapon of grace is the Word of God.

Read 2 Timothy 3:16-17. How does a thorough knowledge and understanding of God's Word help us fight sin?

When we know the Scriptures well, we can distinguish lies from truth. Both the Holy Spirit's whispers and the Devil's accusations can make us aware of our shortcomings and the impossibility of earning favor with God. The difference between what the Holy Spirit does and what the Devil does is the way they use the gospel. The Devil brings up gospel truths to accuse and condemn, whereas the Spirit brings up these truths to convict and to comfort. If you look at your sins and constantly feel condemned, you need to use the Word of God to rebuke the Devil's accusations. Use the Word to remind yourself over and over again that the gospel is true.

Are there any specific Scriptures you have memorized specifically to combat the attacks of the Devil? What are they?

If there are none, read the following verses and identify one you would like to memorize.
John 10:27-28
Romans 1:16-17
Romans 8:1
Romans 8:38-39
Galatians 2:19b-20
1 John 4:15-16

The third weapon of grace is the promise of the new covenant.

Read Hebrews 9:15. How does embracing the new covenant help you deal with your sins?

The three weapons of grace coalesce in our belief in the new covenant. The Scriptures remind us that the old self is dead, nailed to the cross with Jesus Christ. All of our sins—past, present, and future—were paid for in full on the cross of Jesus Christ. We have been sanctified "once for all" (Heb. 10:10). God remembers our sins no more (see Heb. 8:12). And we no longer need to feel shame for those things, because Jesus has completely atoned for those things with His blood. Because Jesus lived a perfect life in obedience to the law, His payment for sin extends to all who repent and trust Him.

When we fight sin, we don't do so in our own power. We fight sin with the weapons grace gives us: the blood of Jesus Christ, the Word of God, and the promise of the new covenant.

IN PRAYER TODAY THANK GOD FOR THE WEAPONS OF GRACE AND GO TO WAR WITH THEM.

Attacking the Roots

The weapons of grace we examined yesterday—the blood of Christ, the Word of God, and the promise of the new covenant—ensure that our war against sin is waged through the knowledge and power of the cross. In that battle of grace-driven effort, we attack the roots of our sin rather than just the branches.

Think carefully about the previous statement. What are the branches of sin?

What is the root of sin?

What's the difference between attacking the branches and attacking the root?

As we saw earlier, grace doesn't tell us to do better. Grace gives us a new heart that's alive to the things of God. That's incredibly important when we go to war against sin because the heart is where behavior originates. Wherever our heart is, our actions will follow. We can manage our behavior until the cows come home and never have a God-loving heart, which is the way the Pharisees lived.

Let's get specific. There's a reason someone might have, for example, a pornography issue. When they return to pornography again and again, it's likely not because they really like sex. God wired us to really like sex. That's just barely scratching the surface of the problem with pornography. Underneath the desire for pleasure is lust, but the reality is that, 9 times out of 10, pornography problems are not just about lust. It runs deeper than that. Lust is a symptom of a more central perversion of the heart.

Men, there's a heart-based reason if you're a miserable husband and father. Women, there's a heart-based reason if you constantly tear down other women and point out their flaws and failures. If the roots are bad, they will produce bad fruit.

Consider some branches of your own sin. Think about some of the most common sins in your life.

Now trace each one back to the heart. What, in your heart, is precipitating those sinful actions?

Why is dealing with the heart the only real way to conquer sin?

Grace-driven effort strives to get to the bottom of sinful behavior, not just manage it. If you're simply managing behavior but not removing the roots of that behavior, the weeds will simply sprout up in another place. You may mow it down for a season, only to see it sprout up again.

Grace-driven effort not only uses the weapons of grace but also attacks the roots. In contrast, moralism attacks just the branches in an effort to subdue behavior. Moralism says, "I've got a pornography issue. Here's what I need to do to stop looking at pornography: install filters, tell a friend who will punch me when I mess up, and maybe even throw away my computer if those steps don't work." There's nothing wrong with safeguards. You won't solve an alcoholic's problems by taking the booze out of his kitchen, but you should still take the booze out of his kitchen. But when all is said and done, if we don't kill the root of sin, we will keep seeing the branches of sin. So grace-driven effort answers the desire, the affections at the heart of pornography or alcoholism. When we apply the weapons of grace, we must ask ourselves, *What exactly are we medicating with those sins? What are we trying to escape or avoid? And how does the gospel fill those needs?*

The use of pornography, for instance, may result from root feelings of shame. As we meditate on the gospel truths that Jesus covers our shame and is not ashamed to call us His brothers and sisters, we cultivate new affections for Him rather than for the deadening substitute of pornography. The abuse of alcohol can result from all kinds of pain: brokenness traced to childhood trauma, patterns developed in early periods of rebellion, or a deep-seated need to escape from personal problems. Even as we seek practical help to avoid drinking, we also need to shine the light of the gospel again and again into these dark recesses of our soul.

Read Ephesians 4:17-24. Where do you see Paul applying the gospel to the root of sin in this passage?

How would your daily approach to sin change if you applied the gospel like this?

The gospel declares that we're reconciled to a perfect Father whose love for us is unwavering and eternal. The gospel wins us to allegiance to Christ, forgiving us of all rebellion and making us prisoners of hope and slaves to righteousness. The gospel brings hope for healing from all manner of hurts. Knowing all the gospel has done for us, we are better equipped to combat idolatry with the real cure, not just superficial behavior modification.

We're seeking heart change, not just conformity to a pattern of religion. We're looking for transformation by the Holy Spirit's power.

PRAY TODAY ABOUT THE CONDITION OF YOUR HEART YOU IDENTIFIED EARLIER. APPLY THE TRUTH OF THE GOSPEL TO YOUR HEART AS YOU SEEK TO PUT ON THE NEW SELF IN CHRIST.

Week 4
The Gospel Pushes You Out

Welcome back to this small-group discussion of *The Explicit Gospel*.

During the previous group experience, you identified one step you could take to grow in holiness by setting your eyes, mind, and heart on Jesus. If you are comfortable, share whether you were able to take that step and what you experienced as a result.

What struck you as new or interesting in week 3 of the workbook?

What emotions do you experience when you hear the term *born again?* How has your understanding of that phrase changed over the course of your life?

When do you experience joy as a follower of Jesus? With what frequency do you experience this joy—rarely, sometimes, often, or every day?

To prepare to view the DVD segment, read aloud Philippians 2:5-8.

> *Make your own attitude that of Christ Jesus,*
> *who, existing in the form of God,*
> *did not consider equality with God*
> *as something to be used for His own advantage.*
> *Instead He emptied Himself*
> *by assuming the form of a slave,*
> *taking on the likeness of men.*
> *And when He had come as a man*
> *in His external form,*
> *He humbled Himself by becoming obedient*
> *to the point of death—*
> *even to death on a cross.*

Watch

Complete the viewer guide below as you view DVD session 4.

A change of _____ leads to a transformation of external action.

Not only are we reconciled to God, but we are also entrusted with the ministry of _____.

We are _____ of Christ.

We are all different in _____.

We are all naturally and intrinsically _____.

All of us have been called by God to be _____ of the gospel.

_____ are always necessary in preaching the gospel.

God is _____, and God is _____, and that's how men are saved.

Transformed hearts lead to transformed lives, which lead to _____ _____ motivated by delight in our God.

We have been set free from believing we are the center of the universe, and that has opened up our hands to _____ well, _____ well, and _____ well.

The motivation behind our heralding and our good works has to be _____.

What's at stake in our motivation is the _____ of God.

All of life is _____.

What we do on a daily basis is to engage at a level that's _____.

Video sessions available for purchase at *lifeway.com/explicitgospel*

Respond

Discuss the DVD segment with your group, using the questions below.

What images come to mind when you hear the word *reconciliation?* What images come to mind when you hear the word *ambassador?*

For what hobbies or passions—movies, sports, food, and so on—are you an enthusiastic evangelist? What makes those hobbies or passions so enjoyable for you?

Have you known people who effectively served as heralds of the gospel? If so, what made them effective?

What obstacles are holding you back from heralding the gospel more regularly and more effectively in your various spheres of life?

What is one step you could take this week toward removing one of those obstacles? If you're comfortable, share that step with the group for increased accountability.

Conclude the group discussion with a time of prayer. Ask the Holy Spirit to reveal people within your sphere of infuence who need to hear the gospel. Ask for opportunities to serve as a herald for those people. If necessary, ask for courage to take advantage of those opportunities.

Suggested Scripture memory for this week: 2 CORINTHIANS 5:21
He made the One who did not know sin to be sin for us, so that we might become the righteousness of God in Him.

Read week 4 and complete the activities before the next group experience.

Is being saved all God expects of us?

Rather than making us lazy bums, the assurance of God's grace is motivational.

The Gospel Pushes You Out

One way the gospel moves us into maturity is to push us outside ourselves. Over and over again in Scripture, we see ways the gospel propels believers outward to meet the needs of the very worst of humanity.

When we're engaged in that mission, we not only find ourselves preaching and demonstrating the gospel to others, but we also find that doing so actually moves us further along in the process of sanctification.

It's a twofold benefit of living in the gospel. When we engage with the hurt, pain, and sorrow of the world around us, God works through us to spread His message and His kingdom. But He also works in us to show us our inadequacies, shortcomings, and fears. We come to see the places where we don't trust God. Engaging the community around us and ministering to its needs reveal to us the remaining bastions of sin in our lives, the areas we refuse to surrender to God.

4.1

The Story of Ephesus

The story of the church in Ephesus gives us a realistic picture of both how the gospel pushes the people of God out and what happens when those same people choose to move on to something other than the gospel. In Acts 19 we see the founding of the church in Ephesus, first by Apollos, influenced by Priscilla and Aquila, and then eventually by Paul. It's pretty spectacular. Apollos went in and taught about Jesus, and the church took off. Paul did miracles and preached the kingdom, and amazing things happened.

Read Acts 19:10. How effective was the gospel in Ephesus, according to this verse?

What was the effect of preaching the gospel?

Read Acts 19:21-41. What effects did the gospel have when it took root in Ephesus?

Everything was changed in this place, thanks to the gospel. The whole socioeconomic climate of the city was different, owing to the pervasive power of the gospel in the culture.

Read Acts 20:29-30. What did Paul prophesy would happen to the church?

The Book of Ephesians is Paul's letter to the Christians in Ephesus, which he wrote from prison in Rome. This letter doesn't specifically indicate what's happening in the city, but then come the letters of 1–2 Timothy. These books record correspondence between Paul and Timothy, who was an elder in Ephesus.

Read 1 Timothy 4:1-10. What does this passage indicate was going on in Ephesus?

It's interesting to note that within a decade of Paul's prophecy in Acts 20, wolves attacked, and false teachers arose. His prediction had come true. Paul then coached Timothy through the Ephesian controversy, commanding him to fight heresy and to instruct the church extensively in the role of the gospel. Paul taught his son in the faith, Timothy, to use the gospel to combat heresies promoted by some who were attempting to change the nature of the gospel.

Then we come to 1–2 John. John was an elder in Ephesus.

Read 1 John 1:8-9. Based on these words, what do you think was happening in Ephesus?

In his letters John appealed for love and grace but also admonished the believers to combat those who felt they had no need to confess or repent of sin. These are glimpses into the stages of the church in Ephesus. In Revelation 2, however, we see a problem that threatened to be the death of that church.

Read Revelation 2:1-5. What were the Ephesians doing well?

What were they doing poorly?

On paper this sounds like a pretty good church. They knew the truth of the gospel and were staunchly committed to good doctrine. But there was a word of warning too: they had abandoned their first love. Here's the big question: What were they doing at first that was so important to resume?

Read Acts 19:18-20. What marked the Ephesian church in the beginning?

Early on, the Ephesians practiced a raw, gritty admission of shortcoming and guilt, but over time the church had become civilized, somewhat cold, and obsessively acute in their doctrinal awareness. In short, they aligned themselves with what was true but lost their missional edge. They had embraced an overly rationalized faith. Their heads were in the right place, but their hearts had not followed. They had the appearance of godliness but denied the power of the gospel to produce radical affection for Jesus, radical repentance from sin, and radical love for a lost world. In the end they were so proud and so far from the Lord that Jesus had to say, "I'm going to remove My light from you if you don't go back and do what you did at first."

Do you see any indications today that churches or believers are denying the power of the gospel?

What about in your own life? What indications show up there?

One of the best ways to see whether the gospel has truly taken root in a church or a person is whether they are being pushed out. Otherwise, isn't it just a collection of knowledge?

PRAY TODAY FOR A RETURN TO YOUR FIRST LOVE. PRAY FOR A GREATER AWARENESS OF THE GOSPEL THAT PUSHES YOU OUT INTO THE WORLD.

Fashioned for Mission

Embracing the gospel means embracing the mission. An abandonment of the mission reveals an abandonment of the gospel. Oh sure, we might still intellectually assent to the basic facts of Jesus' life, death, and resurrection, but we will have lost our first love. Not only that, but we will have denied the very purpose of our creation.

Read Psalm 139:13-16. What, in your own words, is the basic message of this passage?

Why do you think God would be concerned that we know these truths?

How can pressing into God's intimate knowledge and sovereign creativity push you out on mission?

This passage reflects God's sovereignty in every area of life. God knit us together in the womb. He intricately wove our frames. That means He created and wired our external, physical bodies according to the ways He planned to use our lives.

Are you thankful for the way God made your frame? Why or why not?

Have you ever considered how your frame might be made with mission in mind? Why or why not?

Take me, for example. I have always had what adults call a voice that carries. In fact, one of the great ironies of my life is that what I now get paid to do, I once got detention for. I don't possess the ability to whisper. By my design, by my genetic makeup, I am loud. I can't lean over and whisper so that other people in the room can't hear me. I simply don't have that ability. God designed and wired my physical frame—six feet, four inches; two hundred pounds; and gangly—in my mother's womb. This gives me nothing to boast about physically, but it tells me that before I was conceived, God had a plan for my physical makeup that was in keeping with His mission.

Consider again how God specifically made your frame. What are you wired to do for His mission?

What about your internal and emotional self? What qualities do you possess internally that fit you for mission?

Psalm 139:16 tells me that my emotional makeup—the essence of my personality—was placed in there by God. He wired me physically and emotionally to bring Him glory throughout all of my days before I had lived one of them.

There is an intrinsic magnetism in our soul that draws us toward certain things. Psalm 139 reveals that this attraction is God-ordained. God has wired us this way for His purposes. If you like baseball or dancing or reading, it probably has a missional purpose and is not intended just for your own entertainment and enjoyment.

Compare Psalm 139 to Acts 17:24-28. What similarities do you find in those passages?

Besides our external and internal makeup, what else has God done to outfit us for mission?

Not only have we been uniquely wired by God, but we've also been uniquely placed by God. The boundaries of our habitation and the allotted times of our lives were set for us according to God's predetermined plan. We are uniquely wired, and we are uniquely placed.

Think about where you have been uniquely placed. How might you embrace God's sovereign placement of you for mission in the following contexts?

Your job:

Your neighborhood:

Your family:

If we really believe in God's sovereign design, we have to live on purpose. We have to believe that the neighborhood, occupation, cubicle, or chair in which we spend our time is ordained by His design. Then we begin to see our purpose in the world through the lens of how God has wired us and where He has placed us for His glory.

PRAY TODAY, THANKING GOD FOR YOUR EXTERNAL FRAME, YOUR INTERNAL MAKEUP, AND YOUR PLACEMENT FOR HIS MISSION. ASK FOR EYES OF FAITH TO SEE HOW YOU MIGHT BE SENT OUT WHERE YOU ALREADY ARE.

Reflections of the Divine

To be pushed out on mission by the gospel is part of the maturation process in Christ. It's one way the gospel continues to be central in our lives after the initial point of salvation.

As we've seen, God has hardwired His mission into you. He has uniquely formed you, inside and out, and has placed you in a specific context for His glory. So engaging in His mission is linked to identifying with the person God has uniquely made you to be. Doing so is part of the natural progression of being saved by the gospel, which we see in Scripture.

Read Ephesians 2:8-10. What are the three components of the process identified here?

Paul wrote that you're saved by grace through faith to do good works. You can't divorce one from the other two. And those good works you're meant to do were planned specifically for you beforehand. No one else is meant to do the good works you were meant to do, because no one has been created, formed, and positioned in the same way you've been.

Living out God's mission, then, begins right where you are with the person God has created you to be. When you operate from that identity, you're not only doing good things for others but also becoming reflections of the divine, as you were meant to be.

Read Ephesians 5:1-2. Who are you, according to this passage?

In light of who you are, what are you meant to do?

Why do you think it's important to understand that link? What happens when you try to love others without a firm belief in God's love for you?

At some level we all reflect our personal experience, and most of the time that's negative. Statistics clearly tell us that if we've suffered abuse or mistreatment, we're far more likely to perpetuate the same or similar kinds of abuse. We spread what's been spread to us. But the same dynamic works in a gospel-centered manner.

We aren't just meant to go out and love others. We're meant to go as dearly loved children. When we're living in the finished, perfect, and proven love of God in Christ, we're freed to truly love other people. That's what the root of our compassion and care is.

The bad news is that you can't manufacture a sufficient amount of care and compassion on your own. You can't grit your teeth hard enough and scream, "So help me, I will love my neighbor!" It doesn't work that way. In fact, if you're having a hard time loving others, the gospel-centered approach isn't to try harder to love others. Instead, it's to return to and reflect on the extravagant love of God that's been given to you in Christ.

Take a look at your life. What personal experiences are you currently reflecting in your relationships with others?

How might reflecting on the gospel help you better reflect God's love?

All of the things we're called to do in Scripture are great and noble deeds: care for the poor, protect the widow, father the orphans, visit the imprisoned, and so on. But all of them must be rooted in what God has done for us. When we had nothing, He made us rich in Christ. When we were orphans, He brought us into His house. When we were bound by the chains of sin and death, He emancipated us in Christ. That's the impetus and motivation for reaching out to others in His love.

If we try to guilt ourselves into doing good, the end will be temporary. Our hearts will grow cold and bitter. We must be refreshed again and again with what God has done for us in Christ.

Read 2 Corinthians 5:14-21. How are we meant to reflect God's work?

What does it mean to reconcile?

Why do you think Paul referred to Christians as ambassadors in this passage?

An ambassador is someone who simply relays his or her own experience in a foreign context. That's what we do here on earth. All of our good works, which God has prepared for us in advance, are rooted in what we have experienced in the gospel of Christ. When we do good works, we offer others a glimpse into the character of God.

PRAY TODAY THAT ALL OF YOUR GOOD DEEDS WILL BE ROOTED IN THE GOSPEL.

A Response to the Gospel Isn't the Gospel

Scripture identifies imperatives for Christians who want to model the gospel and God's character in the world around them. Feeding the poor, caring for the hurting, adopting orphans, and many other good deeds are marks of disciples of Christ. But we need to be careful to distinguish between the gospel's content and the gospel's implications.

The gospel encompasses God's work, culminating in Christ, to restore all things. It's sometimes tempting to see our good works, whether preaching Scripture or serving meals at a homeless shelter, as God's good news. We need to distinguish between the gospel and our response to the gospel, or we compromise both.

Do you agree with the previous statement? Why do we need to distinguish between the gospel and our response to the gospel?

What happens when we start seeing our good works that respond to the gospel as the gospel itself?

It might seem innocuous enough. The word *gospel* is certainly tossed around enough these days in a variety of ways. But eternity is at stake in what we understand that word to mean. If by the gospel we mean making the world a better place, although the gospel no doubt accomplishes that, we might share food or shelter with someone but fail to offer them the chance to enter the kingdom of God.

We can clearly see the separation between the gospel's content and the gospel's implications in Acts 2.

Read Acts 2:22-24. What was the content of the gospel, according to Peter?

Now read Acts 2:42-47. What were the implications of the gospel, as described in this passage?

All of the things that prompt people to mistakenly say, "This is the gospel" can be found in verses 42-47. What we see in those verses is the beautiful fallout of the proclamation that precedes it. This list reveals the hearers' response to the gospel. Why did they start living in community? Because the gospel had made them a people. Why did they begin to share their goods with one another? Because the gospel had made them a family. Why were they now on mission? Because the gospel had made them a people. Why were they seeing signs and wonders? Because the gospel had made them a people. All of these actions were products of the gospel.

Here's the really tricky part. Almost everyone who subverts the gospel with the results of the gospel didn't start out to do so. Far from it, in fact. They looked at the imperatives in Scripture and observed that for much of the past century of Christian history, the church has walled itself off. We have created fortresses of believers that have little or no impact on our communities.

Their intentions were noble: to demonstrate the gospel in the community in practical ways. But unless a line is clearly drawn between the gospel and its implications, between the message and the response, we inevitably drift away from the explicit gospel.

Why do you think we tend to drift away from the explicit gospel?

Is it possible to do good works in the world around you and still preach the explicit gospel? What are some practical ways you might keep that line firmly fixed between the two as you go out to do good works?

Who do you know who needs to hear the explicit gospel? What is an action you might take that would clearly highlight that gospel?

Believing the news that God is holy, that you are a sinner, and that Christ has reconciled you to God by his life, death, and resurrection justifies you. This is our foundation, our root. The things we read in Acts 2:42-47 are the fruit. They show the building of the home, but they are not the foundation.

If we confuse the gospel with our response to the gospel, we risk drifting into actions that obscure the gospel instead of revealing it. At the end of the day, our hope is not that all the poor on earth will be fed. That's simply not going to happen. I'm not saying we shouldn't feed and rescue the poor; I'm saying that salvation isn't the same as having a full belly.

Making people comfortable on earth before an eternity in hell is tragic.

PRAY TODAY FOR A RENEWED COMMITMENT TO SHARING THE EXPLICIT GOSPEL. ASK FOR THE WISDOM TO KEEP THE LINE CLEAR BETWEEN THE GOSPEL AND THE IMPLICATIONS OF THE GOSPEL.

The Gospel Doesn't Need Saving

As the gospel matures us, it pushes us out into the world to do all the Bible commands us to do in confronting systemic levels of injustice, sorrow, and poverty and in seeking gospel inter- actions with worldly people and powers. But as we do that, we quickly learn that people are offended by the message of Christ's atoning work on the cross.

What is so offensive about the gospel?

Is it a good thing or a bad thing that people are offended by the gospel? Why?

Christ's death on the cross is an indictment of how horrific we are at our core. Nothing is more frustrating to unbelievers than to realize they are broken and sinful, not just by their actions but also by their nature. Most people today find it easy to compare themselves to their neighbors, to somebody they know who "really has issues," or maybe even to a criminal they see on the news and conclude that they are good people. To think of a God who would kill His own Son in order to save them? They can't fathom it. It doesn't penetrate their hearts and minds.

What is an instance when you have seen the gospel offend someone?

Read again from Peter's sermon in Acts 2:22-36. What are some ways Peter might have softened his message?

Why was it important for Peter not to do so?

This was not a seeker-sensitive sermon. Peter didn't shrink back in fear, thinking, *Oh man, this is going to be offensive. How can I make this sound cool to the young Jerusalemites who are here? How can I soften this?* Peter knew if he told them they killed Jesus, they'd get really angry. But he said anyway, "You killed Jesus." Not once but twice (see vv. 23,36).

We will never be able to make Christianity so cool that everybody wants it. Yet this is precisely what we are tempted to do: cut off large swaths of the gospel to make it more palatable to the lost.

Have you ever been tempted to soften the offensive nature of the gospel? In what context? Why do you think you were tempted to make the gospel more "acceptable" at that time?

How did you deal with that temptation?

What might some effects be if you compromised the offensive nature of the explicit gospel?

Every effort to remake the Christian faith leads to wickedness. Every effort to adjust the gospel so that it appears more appealing, more palatable, is foolishness. But ironically, we think we can save Christianity by changing Christianity. We think the gospel needs our help.

But in the urban context of Acts 2, when people all over the ancient world had gathered in Jerusalem, Peter announced, "You killed Him. This majestic one true God of the universe—you crucified Him."

Read Acts 2:37-41. What happened?

How might this reaction bolster your confidence in sharing the explicit gospel?

Peter simply preached the gospel, and people were cut to the core with conviction. They wanted to know, "What do we do in response to this news?" Peter told them, "Repent and get baptized."

What saved them? Their faith. No action brought about their salvation. They hadn't fed any poor people or performed other good deeds. Apart from what Peter said, they hadn't been learning from godly teachers or going to church each week. They simply heard, "God is majestic, and you have sinned, but in Christ you can be reconciled to Him." They were so cut to the heart by the explicit gospel that they responded with saving faith.

Acts 2 highlights the fact that we simply have to tell people the truth of the gospel. There is freedom for us in this. We don't have to explain the gospel perfectly, defend creationism, or argue the falsity of atheism. It's great to have those abilities, but in the end it is God who opens hearts and minds. Our responsibility is to tell people. It's as simple as that. That's the power of the gospel.

THANK GOD TODAY THAT HE BEARS THE RESPONSIBILITY OF OPENING HEARTS. LET THAT FACT ENCOURAGE AND EMBOLDEN YOU TO SPEAK THE WORDS OF THE GOSPEL.

Week 5

The Gospel Holds You to the End

Start

Welcome back to this small-group discussion of *The Explicit Gospel.*

In the previous group experience you identified one step you could take toward removing an obstacle that prevented you from serving as a more effective herald of the gospel. If you are comfortable, share whether you were able to take that step and what you experienced as a result.

What struck you as new or interesting in week 4 of the workbook?

What is your God-given mission in life? How do you know?

How would you summarize our culture's reaction to the gospel of Jesus Christ?

To prepare to view the DVD segment, read aloud Isaiah 40:10-11.

> *Go on up to a high mountain,*
> *O Zion, herald of good news;*
> *lift up your voice with strength,*
> *O Jerusalem, herald of good news;*
> *lift it up, fear not;*
> *say to the cities of Judah,*
> *"Behold your God!"*
> *Behold, the Lord God comes with might,*
> *and his arm rules for him;*
> *behold, his reward is with him,*
> *and his recompense before him.*
> *He will tend his flock like a shepherd;*
> *he will gather the lambs in his arms;*
> *he will carry them in his bosom,*
> *and gently lead those that are with young.*

Watch

Complete the viewer guide below as you view DVD session 5.

As long as your eternal security has your _____ woven into its existence, you're always going to struggle with the _____ you have in God's hands.

The key to feeling safe in the arms of our Father is not to focus on us but to focus on the One who _____ us.

Not only is God infinitely deep in wealth, but when it comes to wisdom and knowledge, God is aware of everything at a _____ level.

God also knows everything at a _____ level.

You cannot put God in your _____.

God owes you _____.

All God's power, wealth, and might are put into saving you in Jesus Christ and _____ you to the end.

People need a picture of God that makes them know they are _____ no matter what.

The gospel _____ us because the coming of Jesus Christ is the objective evidence that God is all in for His glory by _____ you.

Video sessions available for purchase at *lifeway.com/explicitgospel*

Respond

Discuss the DVD segment with your group, using the questions below.

What are your initial reactions to the DVD segment? What did you like? What made you uncomfortable?

In addition to riches, wisdom, and knowledge, what other attributes of God's character and power are identified in Scripture? Consider listing these on a white board or on a large sheet of paper.

Matt said, "You might know that it hurts, you might know that it's hard, you might know that you don't like it," but you can't question what God is doing. Do you agree or disagree? Why?

When have you been tempted to behave as if God were in your debt?

Matt said, "All God's power, wealth, and might are put into saving you in Jesus Christ and sustaining you to the end." What emotions do you experience when you contemplate that truth?

Conclude the group discussion with a time of thanksgiving and praise. Whether silently or aloud, praise God for the elements of His character that you find most worthy of worship. Thank God for the blessings in your life for which you are most thankful.

Suggested Scripture memory for this week: ROMANS 11:33

> Oh, the depth of the riches
> both of the wisdom and the knowledge of God!
> How unsearchable His judgments
> and untraceable His ways!

Read week 5 and complete the activities before the next group experience.

When was the last time you didn't feel like believing the gospel?

Times like those are never far from our minds.

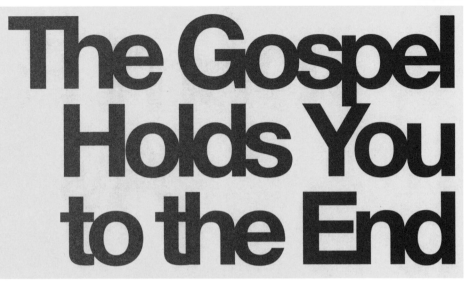

The Gospel Holds You to the End

What was happening? Were you in physical pain? Emotional turmoil? Circumstances mounting against you like waves crashing onto a boat?

These times bring to the surface just how shallow our faith is. Despite what we might say in Sunday School classes, most of us still hold on to the idea that if we have a consistent quiet time and avoid sin, God is going to make our lives easy.

When He doesn't, we feel betrayed and wonder whether the truth of Scripture is really true at all. Thank God that our perseverance in faith is not up to us, because there are many days when we don't feel like believing.

We persevere in our faith not because of our own power to believe but because the gospel holds us to the end.

Don't Fall Away

There are some well-worn statements in churches that have a kernel of truth in them but have been hijacked for wicked purposes. Take, for example, the statement "Once saved, always saved."

Have you ever heard this statement? What were the circumstances?

What do you think the statement means?

Is it true?

I'm sure the first person who said this meant it for good. He or she probably wanted to help people live in confidence, knowing if you've truly been saved from God's wrath and the just punishment for your sin, you will always be saved. Your bad choices won't make you lose what Christ bought for you at the cross.

To put it another way, you can't outsin grace.

But over the years people have looked at statements like this and concluded that once they've been saved, their behavior has no relevance for the Christian life. Because they've walked an aisle, prayed a prayer, and been baptized, they can live in whatever way they want. Truth is, they might not even believe in Jesus anymore, but they've got the salvation issue taken care of just in case.

Read Jude 3-4. In your own words, what were the men doing who are described in verse 4?

Do you think these men thought of themselves as saved?

What is the warning for us in this passage?

The Bible is incredibly realistic about self-deception. Paul explicitly wrote in 2 Corinthians 13:5 to "test yourselves to see if you are in the faith. Examine yourselves. Or do you yourselves not recognize that Jesus Christ is in you?—unless you fail the test." Another terrifying text about self-deception comes in Matthew 7.

Read Matthew 7:21-23. Why were those described in this passage so surprised?

What emotion do you think Jesus meant to inspire with this teaching?

There is a real possibility that we might be hoping in the wrong thing. We might be masquerading as people of faith, only to come to the horrifying realization that we haven't been radically and dramatically seized by the gospel. The people in this passage certainly weren't.

So does God want us to live constantly looking over our shoulders, evaluating everything we do to make sure we really believe?

Not necessarily. If we want to take seriously the commands of Scripture, though, we need to take seriously the warning here, as well as the command to test the validity of our faith. Part of that testing involves honestly determining whether the gospel is maturing us to do good and to grow in holiness. If it's not, we'd better soberly consider whether we really believe in Jesus. As James said in James 2:26, "Just as the body without the spirit is dead, so also faith without works is dead." So test yourself. Look at your life. Are you using the gospel to allow yourself to sin? May it never be so.

Examine your life. Is the gospel producing spiritual maturity and the fruit of good works in your life?

Is there any area of your life in which you're allowing yourself to persist in sin?

In doing this testing, we've got to be careful. No doubt the gospel produces in us good works, but those works must be driven by genuine faith. That's a key difference, because the people of Matthew 7 held up their own good works to Jesus: "Look here! There's got to be some mistake. Look at all the good stuff we've done in Your name!" Apparently that's not enough.

Lots of people do good things. Lots of *lost* people do good things. The road to destruction is packed with them. But the narrow road is marked by faith. Spiritual progress on that road is marked by a growing confidence in Christ's finished work for us, not a growing confidence in our work for Him.

Don't fall away. Renew your confidence in the gospel today—not in yourself and your good works.

PRAY, RENEWING YOUR CONFIDENCE IN THE GOSPEL. THANK GOD FOR THE FINISHED WORK OF CHRIST THAT IS AT WORK IN YOU.

God Works In; We Work Out

It's easy for us to begin trusting in our good works to merit favor before God. Maybe it's so easy because virtually every other area of life works like that. We advance in business through our productivity. We advance in relationships through our networking skills. Even in parenting, though we say our love is unconditional, we often base our love for our kids on whether they keep the bathroom clean and their beds made.

In terms of spiritual maturity and perseverance, though, we must trust in the work of God rather than our work. Paul demonstrated what this kind of trust looks like in two key passages in the Book of Philippians.

Read Philippians 1:6, a verse you studied in week 1. What was Paul confident of in the case of the Philippian believers?

What was the reason for his confidence?

How does Paul's confidence relate to the good works of the Philippians?

The Philippians were good at doing good. They were, in fact, some of Paul's favorite people. But how did he know they would persevere in belief? How did he know someday, because of external pressure or internal doubt, they wouldn't stop believing in the gospel?

It wasn't because of all the good stuff they did. It was because God had started a good work in them. And God always finishes what He starts.

That is a key difference. The good works of the Philippians and of all Christians are the natural progression of God's work through the gospel. Remember Paul's famous verses about the scope of salvation in Ephesians 2:8-10? We are saved by grace through faith to do good works. You can't chop off one of those parts. They go together.

For Christians, good works don't merit God's favor; they demonstrate the salvation Christ won for us at Calvary. They aren't the means of acceptance; they are the natural result of acceptance.

Paul delved into the relationship between these things in Philippians 2.

Read Philippians 2:12. What do you think it means to work out your salvation?

Why must this be done with fear and trembling?

The verb tenses in this verse indicate working at something continuously and unceasingly until it is accomplished. So don't make the mistake of thinking you don't work hard as a Christian. You do. But you work hard in the gospel. That's where verse 13 comes in.

Now read Philippians 2:13. What is the relationship between verses 12 and 13?

Why is it important to read these two verses together?

Taken alone, verse 12 could easily create a bootstraps mentality in us, whereby we pull ourselves up and constantly work for a perpetually unsatisfied slave master. We work tirelessly and unceasingly, only to get up the next day and work more.

Taken alone, verse 13 could easily create in us a spiritual lethargy whereby we simply sit back, let go, and let God. No effort required. We are passive bystanders to Christianity, inanimate objects waiting to be moved by divine hands.

When these verses are taken together, though, we find that both God and we are working.

Reread Philippians 2:12-13 in conjunction with each other. What's the difference between our work and God's work?

Again, our work and God's work aren't the same kind. God's work is the conforming. The transforming. The changing. The prying of those white-knuckled fingers from around our hearts. Our work? Our work is in the arena of faith.

We are to work hard, but we are to work hard at believing. Believing that God is at work in us. That He can conform us through the Holy Spirit to the image of Christ. That He has freed us from being slaves to sin.

What are some ways God is working in your life?

What are some ways you're working out the implications of the gospel in your life?

God works in, and we work out.

WORK HARD AT BELIEVING IN GOD'S WORK IN YOU TODAY. IN PRAYER EMBRACE THE WORK OF GOD IN YOUR HEART.

Suffering According to the Gospel

We've seen that our good works tempt us to abandon our hope in the gospel. But there are other things in life that might tempt us to fall away. One avenue for potential pitfalls is suffering.

People get cancer. They have car accidents. They lose jobs and homes. Bad things happen. It's because of sin that all this stuff occurs. And because we live in a world broken by sin, none of us are immune. The fact that we're not immune is actually one of the things that link us together. Suffering, in one form or another, is common to the whole human experience. The question, then, is not whether you will suffer. The question is what happens when you suffer.

Read Job 1:8-11. What did Satan argue Job's faithfulness to God depended on?

Read Job 2:1-5. What did Satan claim Job's continued faithfulness to God depended on?

Do you see the crux of Satan's argument? He simply couldn't imagine that someone's faithfulness to God depended on something other than circumstances. If circumstances are good, worship goes up. If circumstances are bad, worship goes down or is abandoned. And there is a certain element of truth in that argument.

There's nothing like suffering to reveal what you truly value. Words are cheap. Anyone can worship when there's plenty of money in the bank, health is good, and children are behaving. But suffering is the fire that burns away the fluff. Suffering reveals the authenticity of what we claim to believe. For that reason, one of two things happens during trials: either a person is pushed away from God, or a person is pushed deeper into God and the gospel.

Read the reaction of Job's wife to suffering in Job 1:9. Compare that to Job's response in Job 1:20-22. What differences do you see?

What are some common ways you respond to trials in your life?

Job didn't deny his sadness. He didn't claim the events surrounding him weren't tragic. Yet neither did he cease in his worship of and faithfulness to God. His wife, on the other hand, was ready to call the whole thing off: "Curse God and die!" she said. We don't know what happened to her in the end. But the remainder of the Book of Job records Job's response at a deeper level.

Job asked hard questions. He sought justice from the Lord. He refused to settle for the simple, trite explanations of his friends, who argued that Job was being paid back for sin he had committed. He stubbornly held on to his belief that there was some divine intentionality behind his suffering. But here's an interesting thing about Job's search for answers: he never got them.

Yet Job got something better. The last portion of the Book of Job records that God answered Job out of the whirlwind. We never once find God answering Job's questions, but we find Him revealing Himself—His power, His creativity, and His wisdom.

Why do you think God didn't answer Job's questions?

How do you think God's revelation of Himself to Job relates to the gospel?

Job thought he needed answers, but what he needed much more was a reminder of who God was and is. The same holds true for us. During times of intense suffering, we might think we need answers. We might think we need justice. We might think we even need to be paid back for what we think God has taken from us. We don't. More than anything else, we need the gospel.

What answers did you want from God during times when you have suffered?

What did God give you? Was it answers or something else?

Without the gospel living and working in us, we would surely abandon our belief in God during times of intense sadness and pain. Those are the times when our will runs out. But thankfully, God's grace does not. He still holds on to us even when we don't think we can hold on to Him any longer.

Not only that, but the gospel assures us that God loves us. Purely and completely. No matter what our circumstances might be, we can rest in the historically proven love of God in the gospel. In this way the gospel keeps, encourages, and upholds us during our worst days.

PRAY AS YOU RECALL SOME OF THE WORST DAYS IN YOUR LIFE. BE ENCOURAGED IN THE GOSPEL TODAY AS YOU'RE REMINDED THAT GOD IS FOR YOU.

What Do You Treasure?

One of God's good, gospel-centered purposes in suffering is to reveal in us the things we really treasure. We can fool ourselves into thinking we value Jesus above all else until some of those other things are taken away. At that moment, though, we learn the truth. It's an important truth, because it's both for our good and God's glory that we value Jesus supremely.

Read Matthew 13:44-46. Why did Jesus compare the kingdom of heaven to a treasure and a priceless pearl?

What implications do the actions of the people in these parables have for us today?

Sometimes we treat the gospel of the kingdom not so much like a priceless pearl but like a cubic-zirconium diamond. It sparkles, sure, and it completes the outfit, but we wouldn't be brokenhearted if we lost it because we know deep down that it's not really very valuable.

Jesus didn't die for a cubic zirconium. He died for the greatest cause in the universe—the glory of God. Let me repeat that: Jesus died for the glory of God.

Do you believe Jesus died for the glory of God?

Does that mean He didn't die for you? Why or why not?

From beginning to end, the Scriptures reveal that the foremost desire of God's heart is not our salvation but the glory of His name. God's glory drives the universe; it's why everything exists. This world doesn't exist, spinning and sailing in the universe, so that you and I can be saved but so that God can be glorified in His infinite perfections.

Read the following verses. Record what each one identifies as the means to glorify God.

Exodus 14:14

2 Samuel 7:23

Psalm 106:8

John 7:18

John 12:27-28

1 Corinthians 10:31

Ephesians 1:3-6

2 Thessalonians 1:9-10

You might say this is prooftexting, but this is just the tip of the iceberg. It's found throughout the Bible. That's why the Reformers championed *soli deo gloria* (glory to God alone). The Bible shouts it from every hilltop and rooftop and into every crook and crevice! The glory of God is God's vision and His plan for seeing it fulfilled. Habakkuk 2:14 promises that "the earth will be filled with the knowledge of the Lord's glory, as the waters cover the sea." God's glory is supreme in the Bible because God's plan is for it to be supreme everywhere in the world.

God is always, consistently, and unfailingly acting in His own interests. He's all about His glory. So where do we fit into the picture? The very fact that we object to God's pursuit of His own glory reveals just how self-centered and limited we are. We have a problem with that because we fail to see how wonderful, beautiful, and valuable God's glory actually is.

Opening our eyes wider and wider to the beauty of God in the gospel is part of the gospel's work in us. As God works in us, our capacity to see His greatness increases.

Read Ephesians 1:17-19. How do you see Paul praying for God to increase the people's capacity to know, enjoy, and glorify God?

Have you ever prayed a prayer like that? What were the circumstances?

Perhaps today, in all honesty, you can't say you love God above all things. But maybe you *want* to love God above all things. That desire is evidence of God's work in you. The great news is that God is faithful to enlarge your capacity to treasure Him as He continues to work in you.

He does this by revealing more and more of His greatness, and as He does, He weans you off the menial, temporary pleasures of this world. That's ultimately the way you say no to sin. Because you've seen the greatness of God, you know He is better than anything the world has to offer.

By keeping us to the end, the gospel brings us to greater and greater joy, not in the things of the earth but in God Himself.

PRAY EPHESIANS 1:17-19 FOR YOURSELF TODAY.

Justice Is Coming

The gospel holds us to the end. We're held by grace through the temptations of materialism and sin, as well as through trials and hardship. If left to ourselves, no doubt we would abandon ship at the first sign of trouble. But the gospel changes the core of who we are. To deny the faith, then, is also to deny who we have become in Christ.

God is holding us in the gospel. We'll persevere through this world and all its brokenness and futile attempts at satisfaction, not because of our own strength but because of God's commitment and power to finish in us what He started.

If we understand, then, that there is a destination toward which we are headed, that all of this is actually going somewhere, we can be empowered not only to persevere but also to work for the extension of the gospel and the glory of God in the meantime.

Read Matthew 4:17. What was the core of Jesus' first teachings?

What, in your understanding, is the kingdom of heaven?

How does Jesus' coming relate to the kingdom of heaven?

In the Old Testament God's purpose of choosing the nation of Israel as a people for Himself, calling them out of pagan tribes, and giving them laws for every area of society was to separate them and show a distinction between Israel and the other nations. God did this not so that Israel would be isolated but so that, as they submitted to His laws, they would demonstrate how He intends the world to function.

How did the Israelites do? How well did they pull this off? They stank at it. The Old Testament chronicles their perfecting the art of failure. As they failed time and time again, the prophets among them looked forward to the day when Israel, God's chosen people, would return to their land, repent of their sin, and live according to God's will. In this way Israel was meant to be a light to the nations.

This is important to note: God's people weren't meant to escape the world. God is looking forward to a new heaven and new earth, where everything that has been broken by sin actually works as it's supposed to.

Read Luke 4:16-19. In quoting this passage, what did Jesus demonstrate His mission to be about?

Jesus' miraculous deeds demonstrate His healing of a broken world, revealing that the gospel of the kingdom includes the eradication of disease, the end of death, and the inauguration of a new order. That's what it's going to be like, partially realized in Jesus' first coming, fully realized when He returns.

If you believe in the new heaven and new earth God is creating, how does that change the way you live today?

How does it affect the way you interact with the brokenness of the world?

What are some situations around you that cry out for the light of the gospel?

Read Romans 12:9-21. In one sentence, what was Paul's exhortation in this passage?

How would a belief in the new heaven and new earth fuel the kinds of actions Paul prescribed here?

When we know that justice is coming, that God will set all things right, it means we can be confident in our advocate. We don't have to wring our hands when the wicked prosper. We can endure false accusation and ill treatment. At the same time, we don't act as if it's all OK. We take a stand against evil, but we do so confidently, knowing God is taking notice.

We can wholly love and cling to what is good because we know that justice is coming. The gospel reminds us that God is creating a new earth without the presence of sin. Because He is, we endure, and we endure in faith. We work for the kingdom now while looking forward to the consummation of the kingdom in the future.

PRAY TODAY FOR STRENGTH TO ENDURE. THANK GOD FOR THE CONFIDENCE THAT HE IS MAKING ALL THINGS NEW.

Week 6
The Gospel
Consummation

Start

Welcome back to this small-group discussion of *The Explicit Gospel.*

What have you appreciated most about this study of *The Explicit Gospel?* Why?

What struck you as new or interesting in week 5 of the workbook?

Take another look at Matthew 7:21-23. What emotions do you experience when you hear those words? How do they apply to Christians?

If you are comfortable doing so, talk about a recent time when you experienced suffering. How did that suffering affect your understanding of God and your relationship with Him?

Consider the treasures in your life—possessions, relationships, accomplishments, and so on. Are any of these treasures obstructing your ability to give glory to God? If so, consider sharing the situation with the group in order to work toward a resolution.

To prepare to view the DVD segment, read aloud 1 Corinthians 15:12,16-19.

Now if Christ is proclaimed as raised from the dead, how can some of you say, "There is no resurrection of the dead"? For if the dead are not raised, Christ has not been raised. And if Christ has not been raised, your faith is worthless; you are still in your sins. Therefore, those who have fallen asleep in Christ have also perished. If we have put our hope in Christ for this life only, we should be pitied more than anyone.

Watch

Complete the viewer guide below as you view DVD session 6.

God is committed to conforming you to the image of _____.

God is in the business of _____ and _____ you.

God says, "I am in the process of _____ you."

Sin doesn't just have effects on our spirit; it has effects on our _____ _____.

This physical body is _____.

Our resurrected body will be _____.

We will be unfettered by our physical _____.

Creation itself wants to be _____ _____.

We will live on and reign and worship and rule with God on an earth made _____.

It will be an ever-expanding experience of _____ and an ever-increasing experience of the _____ of God.

No matter how hard things get, I know how it _____.

To know how it ends makes us _____ for the course of sanctification.

All the mercy you need to follow the Lord faithfully today has been given to you _____. There'll be new mercy tomorrow right up until all things are made _____.

The gospel is so much _____ than "Believe this to be saved."

Video sessions available for purchase at *lifeway.com/explicitgospel*

Respond

Discuss the DVD segment with your group, using the questions below.

What emotions did you experience while watching the DVD segment? Why?

Do you view sanctification as exciting or tedious? What question would you most like to have answered about the process of sanctification?

In your own words, summarize Matt's teaching about our physical bodies. What does our culture teach about our physical bodies?

Are you afraid to die? Why or why not?

What question would you most like to have answered about heaven?

Matt said, "All the mercy you need to follow the Lord faithfully today has been given to you today. There'll be new mercy tomorrow right up until all things are made new." Do you believe that to be true? Do you live as if that were true?

Conclude the group discussion by reading aloud Revelation 22:6-21.

Suggested Scripture memory for this week: 2 CORINTHIANS 3:18
We all, with unveiled faces, are looking as in a mirror at the glory of the Lord and are being transformed into the same image from glory to glory; this is from the Lord who is the Spirit.

Read week 6 and complete the activities to conclude your study of *The Explicit Gospel*.

Do the Bible's teachings on the end of time have anything to do with the way we live?

Indeed, the gospel sheds the light of joy and hope on every dimension of life.

The Gospel Consummation

Most of us tend to gravitate toward one of two extremes when thinking about the end times. The first extreme is one of intense focus. From the guy who produces newsletters in his garage about obscure fulfillments of prophecy to the wild-eyed street preacher with a sandwich board reading, "The end is near," there are many believers who passionately dissect every detail of Daniel, Revelation, and other prophetic books of the Bible with the expectation of unlocking mysterious secrets.

The second extreme is one of indifference, avoiding the topic of the end times altogether. We think apocalyptic and prophetic texts are strange, and we get tired of reading about babies being eaten by dragons, stars falling from the sky, and a third of the earth being wiped out. So we opt out of the discussion, claiming that only God knows and He will work it out in the end.

Both of these errors rob us of the gospel-centered approach to the end. From the vantage point of the gospel, the end times are meant to bring about joy and wonder, great expectation and hope as we glimpse the grandeur of God's plan for the cosmos.

The Cosmic Cross

You don't have to be religious to look at the state of the world; conclude that something's gone wrong; and ask, "How did we get here?" We broached that subject earlier in the study when we looked at Romans 8.

Read Romans 8:18-23. Record some insights this passage gives as to what has gone wrong in our world.

Compare that passage to Galatians 4:19 and 1 Thessalonians 5:3. How do these verses fit together?

Nearly everyone has a plan to escape the violence that will accompany the end of time. Every religion has a proposed escape route. Political candidates have plenty of ideas. Talk-show hosts have lots of suggestions. Half of the books in bookstores are self-help books. The need for repair is ever pressing, and would-be repair manuals are easy to come by.

Paul, even as he revealed the brokenness of the world, revealed the fix. He said, "Creation waits with eager longing" (Rom. 8:19, ESV). There's a desire, an expectation within creation that something is going to come that ends the wrong and puts things back together. Our fractured world is begging for redemption.

Paul compared that time to the pains of childbirth to indicate that something is being birthed from brokenness. Our bodies are groaning for redemption; likewise, all of creation cries out in the expectation that what went wrong will be set right. What is the fix? It is to be set free, to experience adoption, and to know redemption. And according to Romans 8, the world is crying out with us.

In what ways do you see our world groaning for redemption?

Read Matthew 27:45-54. Record the immediate effects of the crucifixion.

How do these events relate to the groaning of the world around us?

The cosmic scope of Christ's crucifixion was revealed in the events surrounding it. The sky grew dark. The earth shook. The temple veil was torn in two. Graves popped open, and resurrected bodies danced down the streets of Jerusalem. Clearly, what Christ accomplished on the cross was bigger than our puny minds can fathom. The reaction of the natural order connected Christ's death to a rift in the fabric of creation itself.

Romans 8 gives us a dual perspective of the consequences of the fall: all creation groans in concert with you and me, and the cross is the means of being set free. We receive this double vision in Colossians 1 as well. In that passage Paul clearly talked about the nature of the gospel in regard to individuals.

Read Colossians 1:21-22. How are individual believers reconciled with God?

You and I were reconciled to God by Jesus Christ—specifically, by the cross and resurrection of Jesus Christ, not by any work of our own. Reconciled by Christ, we're no longer enemies with God. The personal relationship Adam and Eve enjoyed with Him has been restored. But Colossians 1 also gives us a wide-angle view, from high above, of this restoration. It's like zooming in on your house on Google Earth and then scanning back out to look at the western hemisphere.

Read Colossians 1:15-19. How does this passage describe the cosmic scope of God's work in the gospel?

This isn't you sitting on Jesus' lap; it isn't individualized. This is unimaginably cosmic. Jesus is the Creator of all things. He is the sustainer of all things. Everything is by Christ, through Christ, and for Christ, from human beings to elephants, from bioluminescent fish in a black cave in South America that no person has ever discovered to microbes underneath a glacier on a distant planet that no person ever will. Christ is Lord over it all. Colossians 1 wants us to see Christ's lordship as very, very *big*. He is certainly not less than our personal Savior and Lord, but he is certainly fathoms, light years, and eons *more* than that.

Why do you think it's important for believers to realize the cosmic scope of the gospel?

To see the gospel consummation, we have to think bigger than ourselves. The idea, for instance, that "the Bible is God's love letter to you" has a kernel of truth to it, but it also illustrates how easily we trade the centrality of God's glory for the centrality of our need. Colossians 1:18 is a dagger in the heart of a human-centered gospel. Christ is the head; Christ is the beginning; Christ is the firstborn; Christ must be preeminent. The explicit gospel, then, magnifies God's glory as it heralds the supremacy of His Son. The gospel of Colossians 1 is epic; it presents a cross that is cosmic.

The scope of Christ's reconciling work on the cross spans the brokenness between man and God and the brokenness between earth and heaven. The cross is the linchpin in God's plan to restore all creation.

That's what we're headed toward in the gospel.

PRAY TODAY FOR DELIVERANCE FROM A HUMAN-CENTERED GOSPEL. ASK GOD TO OPEN YOUR EYES AND HEART TO THE TRUE SCOPE OF WHAT HE IS DOING.

A New Earth

At the time of this writing, the world has its gaze on Japan, where an earthquake rating of 8.9 on the Richter scale and the ensuing tsunami have decimated hundreds of square miles and killed thousands of people. This tragedy is just the latest reminder that something is very wrong. What has happened in Japan is no different from what happens every day in places where weather kills the unprotected, children die of malaria, and doctors diagnose patients with cancer. These events prompt us to groan for deliverance as all creation eagerly awaits its liberation. That liberation is the promise of the gospel.

Read Isaiah 65:17. What is most encouraging to you about this verse?

Compare that passage to Revelation 21:1-2. What similar themes do you see?

Isaiah prompts us to look forward and envision the day when God will create a new heaven and new earth, and all the former things—pain, sorrow, difficulty, and rebellion—will no longer be remembered. John's writing in Revelation 21 shows us that the goal of redemptive history is the restoration of fallen creation as a new heaven and new earth are ushered in.

But here's something worth noting. In Revelation 21 the Greek word for *new* is *kainos*, not *neos*. *Kainos* means *new in nature or in quality,* while *neos* means *new in time or origin.*

What significance does the word *kainos* have for the way you envision Revelation 21?

When this passage employs the phrase "new heaven and new earth," it means a world *renewed,* not a world brand-new. Therefore, what we see in Scripture's vision of the end of redemptive history is not an earth thrown in the trashcan, with its righteous inhabitants escaping to disembodied bliss in the clouds. Rather, it's a restored earth where creation has been reconciled to God. Looking carefully at Revelation 21, we see heaven meeting the new earth; heaven and earth collide into what is new (or renewed), and all things are made new on that new earth. What will that be like?

Do you have any thoughts or dreams as to what the new earth will be like?
When you think of a renewed earth, what comes to mind?

Consider the most beautiful sunset you've ever seen. Even that, in all its spectacular beauty, is not what it was meant to be. That sunset, along with everything else, is broken and is therefore only a pale imitation of the sunsets that once were and the sunsets that one day will be. Can you imagine how amazing the sunsets will be over a restored earth? I don't know if we can. Such a thought is beyond us, this side of heaven.

But the Bible does tell us some wondrous things about the new earth.

Read the following passages. Beside each one, record the aspect of the new earth that it describes.

Isaiah 35:1

Isaiah 65:25

Amos 9:13

Habakkuk 2:14

Which aspect is most meaningful or exciting to you?

Think about it. Slow down and ponder it. If you know somewhere in the world that is renowned for its spectacular views, what you see there is nevertheless broken, and what is to come on the new earth is far beyond what you can fathom or imagine. The work God does in us through the power of the gospel of Jesus' redemptive work is a glorious mystery, a matter of eternal interest to curious angels (see 1 Pet. 1:12). Is it any wonder that those who are redeemed must have a world to match the splendor of salvation?

Read 2 Peter 3:11-13. Is the fire described in this passage good news or bad news? Why?

What is the purpose of that fire?

Because Jesus is making all things new (see Rev. 21:15) and because this passage in 2 Peter 3 tells us we are waiting for a new heaven and earth, we should not see the fire and dissolution Peter speaks of as annihilating creation but as refining it and remaking it. Think about the way a blacksmith heats a piece of metal to soften it before hammering it into shape.

How do you see God preparing you to dwell with Him in the new heaven and earth?

We who trust in Christ are counted righteous in Him; this is our justification. And we're being made righteous through the Spirit's sanctifying work in us so that we will be fit to occupy a sanctified creation. We're declared God's righteousness; Christ is our righteousness (see 2 Cor. 5:21). Therefore, we'll be fit for the land where righteousness dwells.

This is the ultimate fruit of gospel mission, and it's undoubtedly what Jesus was praying for when He prayed for God's kingdom to come in such a way that God's will would be done perfectly on earth as it is done in heaven (see Matt. 6:10). Jesus Himself was the answer to this prayer, inaugurating the kingdom of God through His earthly ministry and testifying that people who placed their faith in Him alone would enjoy the blessing of the kingdom's future consummation.

PRAY THROUGH SOME OF THE ASPECTS OF THE NEW CREATION DESCRIBED IN TODAY'S LESSON, GIVING THANKS FOR WHAT GOD IS DOING TO PREPARE YOU AND ALL BELIEVERS FOR YOUR ULTIMATE HOME.

Resurrected Bodies

The thought of a new earth, a restored earth, is breathtaking. It's arresting. But we can't stop there. Some of us picture human existence in eternity as very ethereal. Everyone looks like a fat little cherub playing a harp, and they float around on clouds in slow motion.

So what will life in the consummated kingdom really be like? When God restores what was broken by the fall and delivers a new heaven and new earth, what will be the role of believers in Christ? There are many possibilities for conjecture; however, we can reasonably ascertain from Scripture that, along with God, we will reign and rule this new creation in resurrected bodies.

Read Romans 8:23. In what ways are you most conscious of your need for bodily redemption?

Children usually don't know their bodies need redemption. Unless they get sick or fall down, they aren't aware they're growing up, only to gradually lose all their strength and vitality. We learn that as we get older. In fact, the point of the final chapter of Ecclesiastes is that our bodies wear out. It doesn't matter how strong our spirits are; Ecclesiastes 12 says a day will come when we will get tired of being alive. Death came with the fall, and all of us are headed in that direction. It doesn't matter how much spinach we eat, how much we exercise, or how wise our life choices are; we are going to die, and our bodies are going to give out.

What kinds of lessons and truths might God reinforce in us through the decay of our bodies?

How should a Christian's approach to bodily decay be different from a non-Christian's?

How can times of sickness and physical pain be seen and used in a redemptive way?

Christians understand that our bodies wear out, because we're waiting for bodies that don't. These new bodies aren't spiritual, ethereal ones. We are awaiting new physical bodies.

Read 1 Corinthians 15:35-58. What part of Paul's description of the new body is most meaningful to you? Why?

Verses 35-46 suggest that no matter how impressive we make our bodies through a healthful diet, rigorous exercise, adequate sleep, and effective stress management, the body is just a seed, not the tree or the flower. Regardless of how strong we make our bodies, that power is fleeting.

In verses 47-49 Paul compared and contrasted the man of dust, Adam, with the Man of heaven, Jesus Christ. All of us, having been born of a woman, are born in the image of our first father, Adam. So like him, each one of us has preferred creation to the Creator, has believed that we're smarter than God, and has failed to acknowledge Him. And if Christ delays His second coming, each one of us will die the death of Adam.

Remember that there was no death until sin was introduced into the cosmos. When the fall occurred, death began to reign. You and I are going to die physically, and even if Christ returns before we do, we're still going to need a replacement for our perishable bodies. We'll need to put on an imperishable body, purchased for us by the Man of heaven. We'll receive new bodies like Christ's resurrection body. Then, whereas we once lived as broken images of God, at that time we'll bear the image of Jesus, the perfect image of the invisible God. The brokenness present in each of us will be mended forever, and our eternal, princely bodies will replace our aging flesh.

Read 1 Corinthians 15:54-57. According to Paul, when will death no longer sting?

This text can be used shoddily at funerals. Just inches from an occupied casket, preachers shout, "Where is your sting, O death?" I always want to shout back, "It's right there! There's the sting!"

First Corinthians 15 tells us that death loses its sting when it's swallowed up in victory and can no longer create mourning. It's when we put on the imperishable. So at funerals we mourn, and we hurt; death stings, and there is real loss. This text, when rightly used at a funeral, should point us to the hope of the day when death won't sting any longer.

In that day Christ's victory over death will be tangible, palpable, and visceral. We'll receive new bodies that are powered by the Spirit and capable of feats unimaginable by our present, dimly lit minds. We'll be made fit to swim in God's earth-covering glory. It's likely that our resurrected bodies will be like Jesus' resurrected body. His glorified body perhaps foreshadows ours.

Our resurrected bodies are another implication of the explicit gospel. For if God justifies us, He will glorify us as well (see Rom. 8:30). Count on it.

PRAY TODAY ABOUT YOUR PHYSICAL ACHES AND PAINS, PRAISING GOD THAT THEY REMIND YOU THAT THE IMPERISHABLE IS COMING SOON.

Immanuel

The gospel consummation promises a restored earth—a creation functioning to its full capacity exactly how God designed it. The gospel consummation promises resurrected bodies—men and women functioning to their full capacity, exactly the way God designed them. But there's something else in John's great vision of the future.

Read Revelation 21:3-4. What is significant about the fact that "God's dwelling is with humanity" (v. 3)?

What does that indicate about the nature of our relationship with God at the consummation of all things?

In these few simple words we find the profound destiny for all those Jesus has purchased with His blood. We find absolute and complete intimacy with God. In this is the fulfillment of every statement throughout Scripture that promises the fullness of joy in God's presence (see, for example, Ps. 16:11).

The essence of eternal life is God Himself. Eternal joy can't be viewed, much less experienced, apart from the very foundation of joy. That's God.

Read John 17:3. According to Jesus, what is eternal life?

Is that how you would have previously defined eternal life? Why or why not?

Revelation 21 contains the fulfillment of God's mission, the mission that began when Adam and Eve decided a piece of fruit was better than a perfect relationship with the God of the cosmos. In Exodus 25 God instructed Moses to take up an offering from the people in order to construct a tabernacle. In verse 8 God's desire was clear: "They are to make a sanctuary for Me so that I may dwell among them."

The next four chapters in Exodus detail an elaborate set of instructions for building this sanctuary. The verses go to exhausting ends to make sure the proper materials were used, the measurements were just right, and those ministering there wore the right clothes.

Here's the conclusion: God wants to dwell with His people, to be known by them, and to give them the great gift of knowing Him. But because of their sin, there are barriers to that relational intimacy. The gospel changes all that.

Read John 1:14. How does this text about Jesus relate to God's desire in commanding Moses to build the tabernacle?

A little language study reveals that the words "took up residence" literally mean *pitched His tent*. It's an allusion to God's dwelling among the Israelites. It's God saying, "You made a tent with a lot of curtains. But that was only meant to point you forward to this moment when I'm going to be with you bodily through My Son." God took up residence among His people when the Word was made flesh.

Read Romans 5:1-2. What has Jesus' death gained for us?

How does that truth relate to the image of the tabernacle?

A long time ago access to God was severely limited. Only the high priest could go into God's direct presence, and he could go only once a year. But now the gospel has provided access for all. All have the opportunity to be with God—to know Him and the fullness of joy that comes with Him. That's what the gospel promises.

It's great that on the new earth we won't need tissues. Or pain medications. Or hearses. But this trumps all: on that day we will have God because He made us His treasured possession in the gospel.

Read 1 Corinthians 13:12. What is the difference between the way we know God now and the way we will know and experience Him then?

What do you think the implications will be for your relationship with Him?

This passage captures our imaginations. Consider how well God knows you now. He knows the number of hairs on your head. He has ordered your steps. He knit you together in your mother's womb. He knows everything hidden in the secret places of your heart.

Now consider knowing God like that. This isn't the stuff of a 15-minute quiet time. This is pure, undiluted glory. This is the promise of the gospel: to give us the most immense pleasure imaginable, to fully know God as He dwells with us.

THANK GOD FOR THE INCREDIBLE PRIVILEGE THAT AWAITS YOU. LOOK FORWARD TO THE DAY WHEN YOUR RELATIONSHIP WITH HIM WILL NO LONGER BE MARRED BY SIN AND YOU WILL DWELL IN HIS PRESENCE.

A New Way to Live

The vision is epic; the consummation of the gospel includes all things in heaven and earth. As Paul said in Ephesians 1:10, God's aim is "to bring everything together in the Messiah, both things in heaven and things on earth in Him."

It should be clear by this point that the gospel doesn't make you lazy. It pushes you out into a very specific way of living. We began this journey in 1 Corinthians 15, where Paul reminded us that the gospel is not just the means by which you are saved but also the center of all of life and creation. As we conclude our study by focusing on the end of all things, let's turn back to Paul's conclusion of 1 Corinthians 15.

Read 1 Corinthians 15:58. In your own words, what did Paul exhort the Corinthians to do?

Which part of his charge is currently most meaningful to you? Why?

The first word of this verse, *therefore*, points us back to what Paul expounded on earlier in the chapter. All of these great truths—this life is perishable, these bodies are seeds, and someday the corruptible will be clothed with incorruptibility and immortality—dramatically change the way we see and live in the world.

Specifically, Paul exhorted Christians to "be steadfast, immovable, always excelling in the Lord's work." We're much more willing to serve, sacrifice, and endure discomfort because we know this broken life is momentary. We see this sentiment throughout Paul's writings.

Read 2 Corinthians 4:16-18. How did Paul encourage his readers not to give up?

How does focusing on what is unseen motivate people to do the things Paul listed in 1 Corinthians 15:58?

Everyone views the world through a certain set of lenses, formed by our personal experiences. These lenses might color the world around us with cynicism, pain, or hope. But when we come to Christ, He enables us to see everything differently—through the lens of the gospel. Through the lens of the gospel, we focus on what is unseen, believing things aren't always going to be this way.

What are some circumstances or conditions in your life that you look forward to leaving behind?

How is the gospel giving you hope to look at these things in a different way?

When we see life in the here and now as momentary and our physical bodies as seeds that must die as a precursor to being raised with the risen Christ, the result is boldness for Jesus. A Christian doesn't have to live with the fatalism or hedonism that results when we see our lives in terms of "This life is all there is, so I've got to maximize my pleasure, comfort, and joy right now. I need to experience all the life I can now."

In short, when we are immersed in the gospel of Christ, we are willing to lose our lives because our focus is in a different place.

Read Mark 8:34-38. What happens to those who want to save their lives?

What happens to those who lose their lives?

What argument did Jesus make in verses 36-37 for losing your life for His sake?

The Bible clearly says the quickest way to lose your life is to try to save it, and the way to save your life is to lose it. But don't miss this: losing your life for Jesus' sake is only the first step. It's the means to the end of saving your life. Sure, doing the things Paul commanded might look like loss if your focus is on the temporal. But if you begin to see the cosmic scope of the gospel, what God is up to through all of history, you begin to see that whatever you lose is paltry compared to what you gain.

You can move forward in the gospel. You can persevere in the gospel. You can pursue holiness in the gospel. And you can do so because you are focused on the unseen, looking forward to the consummation of all things under the headship of Christ.

This is where you look in hope. This is what you pray for. This is what you long for when you grow weary of this broken world. This is why you yearn for Jesus' coming. This is why John wrapped up his revelation by saying, "Come, Lord Jesus!" (Rev. 22:20). You can practically hear his broken breathlessness.

The gospel is so much bigger than we've imagined. It's huge. It's not just about God's forgiving us of sins and giving us eternal life. It's also about what we're being forgiven for and what eternal life is like. The Scriptures show us that Christ's atoning work is good news for fallen creation. All of fallen creation. Through the good news of Jesus' life, death, and resurrection, we know the gospel isn't just of first importance (see 1 Cor. 15:3) but of all importance. It's imperative that the gospel we espouse and share takes the shape of the Scripture's epic vision of God's redemptive plan. It's imperative that we embrace a gospel that is scaled to the glory of God.

How is your view of the gospel bigger now than when you began this study?

The gospel is good news. It's great news. It's central news. Preach the explicit gospel to yourself today. Then, when you wake up tomorrow, do it all over again.

PRAY TODAY, THANKING GOD FOR ALL HE IS DOING IN YOU AND IN THE UNIVERSE THROUGH HIS EXPLICIT GOSPEL.

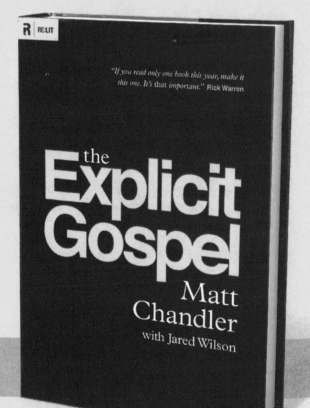